The Inner Sanctum
of Puritan Piety

John Flavel (1628-1691)

The Inner Sanctum of Puritan Piety

John Flavel's Doctrine of Mystical Union with Christ

J. Stephen Yuille

REFORMATION HERITAGE BOOKS
Grand Rapids, Michigan

2007

© 2007 by J. Stephen Yuille

Published by
Reformation Heritage Books
2965 Leonard St., NE
Grand Rapids, MI 49525
616-977-0599 / Fax: 616-285-3246
e-mail: orders@heritagebooks.org
website: www.heritagebooks.org

ISBN 978-1-60178-017-1

Library of Congress Cataloging-in-Publication Data

Yuille, J. Stephen, 1968-
   The inner sanctum of Puritan piety : John Flavel's doctrine of mystical
union with Christ / by J. Stephen Yuille.
      p. cm.
   Includes bibliographical references and index.
   ISBN 978-1-60178-017-1 (pbk. : alk. paper)
   1. Mystical union--History of doctrines. 2. Puritans--Doctrines. 3.
Flavel, John, 1630?-1691. I. Title.
   BX9323.Y85 2007
   248.2'2092--dc22
                              2007013363

*For additional Reformed literature, both new and used, request a free
book list from Reformation Heritage Books at the above address.*

For Laura

Contents

Foreword

In the recent recovery of the theology of the transatlantic Puritan movement, which has been underway since the 1950s, it is interesting to note which authors have been at the center of this recovery. John Owen and Richard Baxter have, in particular, been the focus of attention, and study of the one who might be called the last of the Puritans, Jonathan Edwards, has become an academic industry in its own right.

But if Edwards be regarded as the last of the Puritan theologians—and there are contemporary scholars who would dispute this—then the movement spanned close to two hundred years, beginning in England in the 1560s and ending in New England with the death of Edwards in 1758. As such, it is hardly fair to consider the three Puritan thinkers named above as the only figures worthy of study. They may have been representative in many ways and, in the case of Owen and Edwards, the most brilliant representatives of this remarkable history-shaping body of Christians, but other Puritan theologians deservedly need to be studied.

For this and other reasons that will become obvious in the course of this book, this study of John Flavel on union with Christ is indeed a welcome one. Flavel was widely read in his own day and in the years following his death. The story is told, for instance, of a man in Flavel's lifetime who came across Flavel's *Keeping the Heart* in a London bookshop. "What fanatic was he who made this book?" he exclaimed as he perused its contents. The owner of the shop, though, convinced the man to buy the book with a promise that he would give him a refund if the man continued to dislike the book. A month or so later the man returned, but he had been deeply changed by the book. As he told the bookseller, "Sir, I most heartily thank you for putting this book into my hands;

I bless God that moved you to do it, for it hath saved my soul; blessed be God that ever I came into your shop."[1]

And in the following century, a good number of the leaders and believers in the evangelical revivals that swept British society on both sides of the Atlantic were deeply impacted by Flavel. George Whitefield ranked his works alongside those of John Bunyan (1628-1688) and Matthew Henry (1662-1714) for spiritual usefulness. Many of those converted under the ministry of the Virginia Presbyterian Samuel Davies (1723-1761) were ardent readers of, among other Puritan works, the books of Flavel.[2] And the Yorkshire Baptist leader John Fawcett (1740-1817), who played a significant role in the revival of the Baptist cause in northern England, was deeply attached to Flavel's works, an attachment that helped him to break free from the Hyper-Calvinism then regnant in that part of the country.[3] Rightly did Flavel say: "Though ministers die, yet their words live; their words take hold of men when they are in the dust (Zech. 1:6)."[4]

What all of these readers and others in the eighteenth and nineteenth centuries especially appreciated in Flavel was the fact that the Puritan divine, in the words of Iain Murray, was "one well fitted to lead us in such experimental subjects as communion with God, prayer and the life of faith."[5] These spiritual subjects lay at the very heart of the Puritan movement, for the Puritans were preeminently interested in the walk of faith, the life of prayer, and the Spirit's Christ-centered enabling of these two central aspects of true Christianity. The subject that Dr. Yuille has therefore chosen to focus on

---

1. Iain Murray, "John Flavel," *The Banner of Truth*, 60 (1968): 3.

2. Murray, "John Flavel," 3-4.

3. John Fawcett, Jr., *An Account of the Life, Ministry, and Writings of the late Rev. John Fawcett, D.D.* (London: Baldwin, Cradock, and Joy, 1818), 11-12.

4. Cited in Murray, "John Flavel," 10.

5. Murray, "John Flavel," 7.

in this study of Flavel's thought, union with Christ, is one that is at the very center of this Puritan's entire ministry.

May the perusal of these pages have a revivifying effect similar to that of bygone days and that for the glory of the One whom Flavel delighted in calling the God-Man, his Lord and ours.

—Michael A. G. Haykin

Dundas, Ontario
March 4, 2007

Preface

When I first met Dr. Anthony Lane at London School of Theology to discuss my proposed Ph.D. research, he encouraged me to narrow my focus. I had naively planned to study the significance of filial fear within the broadly defined realm of English Puritanism. He suggested that I limit my research to just one Puritan. Without too much deliberation, I narrowed the candidates to two: George Swinnock and John Flavel. I eventually settled upon Swinnock. Yet, as I studied Swinnock, I nurtured a secret desire to return one day to Flavel. That day came last year.

As I immersed myself in Flavel's writings, I was immediately struck by his theological precision and pastoral fervor. These are nowhere more evident than in his handling of the doctrine of the believer's mystical union with Christ. Years ago, Dr. Martyn Lloyd-Jones summed up his personal delight in this doctrine as follows: "If you have got hold of this idea [i.e., mystical union with Christ] you will have discovered the most glorious truth you will ever know in your life." Without question, Flavel had a firm hold of it, and it was indeed "glorious" to him. It is no exaggeration to say that it is the key that unlocks the door to the inner sanctum of his piety.

In the following pages, I seek to unfold what Flavel has to say about this glorious subject. I have arranged his insights according to eleven themes, taking the reader from the foundation through the implications to the culmination of the believer's mystical union with Christ. My prayer is that this survey will impart to you a deeper appreciation of what it means to be "in Christ."

— J. Stephen Yuille

INTRODUCTION

During the Plague of London in 1665, a small group of dissenting Christians gathered illegally at a private house to pray.[1] Without warning, soldiers entered and arrested a number of the participants. An old non-conformist minister, Richard Flavel, and his wife were among those arrested. Sadly, they contracted the plague while in prison, and died shortly after their release.

All knowledge of this godly couple would undoubtedly be lost to the pages of history if not for the birth of their son, John, in 1627.[2] At some point during his youth, John Flavel was converted to Christ. By his own account, he had been "carried away so many years in the course of this world," but God "roused" his soul "out of that deep oblivion and deadly slumber."[3] After completing grammar school, he studied at University College, Oxford. At age twenty-three, he entered his first pastorate at Diptford in the county of Devon. Six years later, he moved to Dartmouth in the same county. One of his church members provides the following account of his ministry:

---

1. In 1662, Parliament passed an Act of Uniformity, according to which all who had not received Episcopal ordination had to be re-ordained by bishops. In addition, ministers had to declare their consent to the entire Book of Common Prayer and their rejection of the Solemn League and Covenant. As a result, approximately 2,000 ministers left the Church of England. They became known as "Dissenters" or "Non-conformists."

2. For additional details of his life, see *The Life of the Late Rev. Mr. John Flavel, Minister of Dartmouth* in *The Works of John Flavel* (London: W. Baynes and Son, 1820; rpt., London: Banner of Truth, 1968), I: i-xvi; and *Dictionary of National Biography*, ed. S. Lee (London: Smith, Elder & Co., 1909).

3. Flavel, *Works*, II:483-84.

I could say much, though not enough, of the excellency of his preaching; of his seasonable, suitable and spiritual matter; of his plain expositions of scripture, his taking method, his genuine and natural deductions, his convincing arguments, his clear and powerful demonstrations, his heart-searching applications, and his comfortable supports to those that were afflicted in conscience. In short that person must have a very soft head, or a very hard heart, or both, that could sit under his ministry unaffected.[4]

Regrettably, Flavel's public ministry ceased for a time with the issuing of the Act of Uniformity in 1662. For several years, he continued to live in Dartmouth, meeting secretly with church members in order to preach the Scriptures and administer the sacraments. When the Oxford Act prohibited all non-conformist ministers from living within five miles of towns that sent representatives to Parliament, Flavel settled at a nearby village. His people ventured to hear him preach on the Lord's day in private homes or wooded areas, and he slipped regularly into Dartmouth to visit them. This clandestine ministry continued until the political indulgence of 1687 when the authorities permitted him to resume his public ministry.[5] He enjoyed this liberty until his death four years later at age sixty-four.

Flavel was a prolific preacher and writer—his collected works fill six volumes.[6] At times, he is polemical and controversial.[7] More often than not, however, he is doctrinal and pastoral. This emphasis is seen in his twofold approach

---

4. As quoted in Flavel, *Works*, I:vi. For Flavel's thoughts on the pastoral ministry, see *The Character of an Evangelical Pastor Drawn by Christ*, *Works*, VI:564-85.

5. For Flavel's enthusiastic support of the coronation of William III, Prince of Orange, see *Works*, IV:6-16, VI:545-63.

6. For a list of his complete works, see Bibliography.

7. This is evident in his treatises on antinomianism (*Works*, III:413-591) and popery (*Works*, IV:307-35, 557-86).

to preaching: exposition and application.[8] Repeatedly, Flavel follows this simple method, deriving his doctrines from Scripture, and then encouraging his readers to pursue a heartfelt application of those doctrines to the soul.

This "affective" theology places him firmly within the realm of Puritanism—what J. I. Packer calls "a spiritual movement, passionately concerned with God and godliness."[9] Over the years, many doctrinal systems and theological paradigms have been labeled the *Sine Qua Non* of Puritanism.[10] However, a central theme that is often overlooked is

8. For a helpful treatment of Puritan preaching, see Peter Lewis, *The Genius of Puritanism* (Morgan: Soli Deo Gloria, 1996). His analysis is divided into five sections: the Dignity of Preaching, the Necessity of Preaching, the Demands of Preaching, the Character of Preaching, and the Content of Preaching.

9. J. I. Packer, *A Quest for Godliness: The Puritan Vision of the Christian Life* (Wheaton: Crossway Books, 1990), 28. For additional definitions of Puritanism, see Ian Breward, "The Abolition of Puritanism," *Journal of Religious History* 7 (1972): 20-34; Paul Christianson, "Reformers and the Church of England under Elizabeth I and the Early Stuarts," *Journal of Ecclesiastical History* 31 (1980): 463-82; Patrick Collinson, "A Comment: Concerning the Name Puritan," *Journal of Ecclesiastical History* 31 (1980): 483-88; Michael Finlayson, "Puritanism and Puritans: Labels or Libels?" *Canadian Journal of History* 8 (1973): 203-23; Basil Hall, "Puritanism: The Problem of Definition" in *Humanists and Protestants: 1500-1900* (Edinburgh: T & T Clark, 1990), 237-54; Christopher Hill, *Society and Puritanism in Pre-Revolutionary England* (London: Panther Books, 1969), 15-30; Martyn Lloyd-Jones, *The Puritans: Their Origins and Successors* (Edinburgh: Banner of Truth, 2002), 237-59; and Leonard Trinterud, "The Origins of Puritanism," *Church History* 20 (1951): 37-57.

10. Michael McGiffert believes that the Puritans were marked by a predilection for covenant theology in "The Perkinsian Moment of Federal Theology," *Calvin Theological Journal* 29 (1994): 117-48. John Coolidge sees their position on the sufficiency of Scripture as pivotal in *The Pauline Renaissance in England: Puritanism and the Bible* (Oxford: Clarendon Press, 1970). J. Sears McGee views their approach to the law as foundational in *The Godly Man in Stuart England: Anglicans, Puritans, and the Two Tables, 1620-1670* (Yale University Press, 1976).

the believer's mystical union with Christ.[11] The Puritans derive great delight from this doctrine and, therefore, dedicate countless pages to extolling its virtues.[12] This is certainly the case with Flavel, who asks:

> How transcendently glorious is the advancement of believers, by their union with the Lord of glory? This also is an admirable and astonishing mystery; it is the highest dignity of which our *nature* is capable, to be *hypostatically* united; and the greatest glory of which our *persons* are capable is to be *mystically* united to this Lord of glory; to be bone of his bone, and flesh of his flesh. O what is this! Christian, dost thou know and believe all this, and thy heart not burn within thee in love to Christ?[13]

This motif permeates Flavel's works. Whether directly or indirectly, he is constantly handling this "admirable and astonishing mystery." My purpose in this book is simply to consider what Flavel says. My hope is that this discussion will, in turn, contribute to a greater admiration for this pastor-theologian, a greater understanding of Puritan spirituality, a greater appreciation of what it means to be "mystically united to the Lord of glory," and a greater burning of the heart "in love to Christ."

Robert Kendall points to their "experimental" predestinarianism in *Calvin and English Calvinism to 1649* (Oxford University Press, 1979).

11. For an excellent overview of this theme within Puritanism, see R. Tudor Jones, "Union with Christ: The Existential Nerve of Puritan Piety," *Tyndale Bulletin* 41 (1990): 186-208.

12. In this way, Flavel (and the Puritans in general) follow Calvin's lead. As Howard Hageman observes, "If we wish to discuss the spirituality of Calvin, this must be our starting point, the mystical union with Christ" ("Reformed Spirituality" in *Protestant Spiritual Traditions*, ed. F. C. Senn [New York: Paulist, 1986], 61). According to Charles Partee, union with Christ is the "central dogma" of Calvin's *Institutes* ("Calvin's Central Dogma Again," *Sixteenth Century Journal* XVIII [1987]: 191-99).

13. Flavel, *Works*, II:239.

Chapter 1

────────────•»(●)«•────────────

THE COVENANT OF REDEMPTION

The starting-point for Flavel's doctrine of the believer's mystical union with Christ is his covenant theology. In simple terms, covenant theology is a paradigm for interpreting Scripture that arose to prominence in the sixteenth and seventeenth centuries, finding its clearest expression in the publication of the *Westminster Confession of Faith* (hereafter *WCF*) in 1647. Its most distinguishing feature is the emphasis it places on the continuity of God's revelation in all ages, focusing upon God's gracious plan to save His people in Christ. A detailed account of the various factors involved in the development of covenant theology is well beyond the scope of this chapter.[1] My purpose is merely to highlight the major tenets inherent to Flavel's thinking on the subject.

The Covenant Theology of John Calvin

With that in view, we begin with John Calvin. In doing so, I am not suggesting for one moment that Calvin is the father of covenant theology. I am, however, acknowledging his profound impact upon English Puritanism. While recognizing differences between the Old and New Testaments, Calvin

---

1. For Robert Letham's thesis that covenant theology emerged from factors present within Reformed theology from the very start, see "The Foedus Operum: Some Factors Accounting For Its Development," *Sixteenth Century Journal* XIV (1983): 457-67. He identifies four internal factors: (1) its stress on the unity of the covenant of grace in all ages; (2) its stress on the unity of the law; (3) its view of the Decalogue in covenantal terms; and (4) its view of creation in a covenantal framework.

sees continuity between the two under one covenant of grace.[2] He states, "I freely admit the differences in Scripture, to which attention is called, but in such a way as not to detract from its established unity.... Those chief differences... pertain to the manner of dispensation rather than to the substance.... In this way there will be nothing to hinder the promises of the Old and New Testaments from remaining the same, nor from having the same foundation of these very promises, Christ!"[3] As Peter Lillback notes, Calvin's conviction leads him to use the expression "New Covenant" in two distinct senses.[4] First, the New Covenant is the gospel era,

---

2. Some scholars argue that covenant theology is totally absent from Calvin. Perry Miller popularized the idea that it was the Puritans who developed covenant theology in response to perceived deficiencies in Calvin's theological system. By "deficiencies," Miller has in mind Calvin's concept of God's absolute sovereignty, which fails to provide individuals with any motive for moral behavior or any ground for personal assurance (*The New England Mind: The Seventeenth Century* [Harvard University Press, 1963], 366-74). The Puritans remedied these "deficiencies" by creating a covenant theology that stressed human duty. For Miller, Calvin knew nothing of any such system. For similar views, see Christopher Hill, *Society and Puritanism in Pre-Revolutionary England* (London: Panther Books, 1969); and Norman Pettit, *The Heart Prepared: Grace and Conversion in Puritan Spiritual Life* (Middletown: Wesleyan University Press, 1989). Miller's thesis is certainly open to criticism. George Marsden, for example, states, "As for the thesis that the covenant of grace represented a revision of Calvinism, Miller has created a myth that has been so elegantly presented and widely repeated that it will be difficult to destroy" ("Perry Miller's Rehabilitation of the Puritans: A Critique" in *Reckoning With the Past: Historical Essays on American Evangelicalism from the Institute for the Study of American Evangelicals*, ed. D. G. Hart [Grand Rapids: Baker Books, 1995], 38). For a full treatment of this subject, see Peter Lillback, *The Binding of God: Calvin's Role in the Development of Covenant Theology* (Grand Rapids: Baker Books, 2001).

3. John Calvin, *Institutes of Christian Religion* in *The Library of Christian Classics: Vol. XX-XXI*, ed. J. T. McNeill (Philadelphia: Westminster Press, 1960), II.XI.1.

4. Lillback, *Binding of God*, 158.

inaugurated by Christ's redemptive work. In this sense, it is different from the Old Covenant. Second, the New Covenant is "the saving relationship between God and his elect throughout the ages. It either looked forward in promise to Christ's coming or it harks back to his accomplishment of redemption."[5] In this sense, it includes the Old Covenant.[6]

This "saving relationship between God and his elect" begins with God's promise in Genesis 3:15, where He says, "And I will put enmity between thee and the woman, and between thy seed and her seed; it shall bruise thy head, and thou shalt bruise his heel." God progressively develops that redemptive promise in subsequent covenants until the arrival of the seed of the woman: Christ. As Calvin explains:

> The Lord held to this orderly plan in administering the covenant of his mercy: as the day of full revelation approached with the passing of time, the more he increased each day the brightness of its manifestation. Accordingly, at the beginning when the first promise of salvation was given to Adam [Gen. 3:15] it glowed like a feeble spark. Then, as it was added to, the light grew in fullness, breaking forth increasingly and shedding its radiance more widely. At last—when all the clouds were dispersed—Christ, the Sun of Righteousness, fully illumined the whole earth.[7]

According to Calvin, therefore, the one covenant of mercy (or grace) encompasses all of God's people throughout history. It is revealed and administered progressively from Adam to Christ. As Anthony Hoekema observes, it is for Calvin "the thread which ties salvation history together. God saves

---

5. Lillback, *Binding of God*, 158.

6. Flavel agrees with Calvin that the old and new covenants "are essentially but one covenant." *Works*, III:503. For Flavel's view of the Mosaic Law as a covenant of grace, see *Vindiciae Legis et Foederis; or, A Reply to Mr. Philip Cary's Solemn Call*, *Works*, VI:318-77.

7. Calvin, *Institutes*, II.X.20.

his people by means of the covenant of grace which, though it passes through various historical phases, is basically one."[8]

The Covenant Theology of the Westminster Divines

In his discussion of the covenant of grace, Calvin never speaks of a covenant of works. That has led many people to conclude that he did not believe that there was such a thing. However, Calvin's acceptance of the federal headship of Adam and Christ seems to point to the opposite conclusion.[9] He writes, "Accordingly, our Lord came forth as true man and took the person and the name of Adam in order to take Adam's place in obeying the Father, to present our flesh as the price of satisfaction to God's righteous judgment, and, in the same flesh, to pay the penalty that we had deserved."[10]

---

8. Anthony Hoekema, "The Covenant of Grace in Calvin's Teaching," *Calvin Theological Journal* 2 (1967): 139. Flavel shares Calvin's view of progressive revelation, stating, "It is worthy our observation, how God made a gradual discovery of Christ from Adam, down along to the New Testament times. It was revealed to Adam, that he should be the *seed of the woman*, but not of what *nation*, till Abraham's time; nor of what *tribe*, till Jacob; nor of what *sex* and *family*, till David; nor that he should be born of a virgin, till Isaiah; nor in what *town*, till Micah" (*Works*, VI:88-89).

9. Holmes Rolston argues that the Puritans altered Calvin's view of humanity's state in innocence in *John Calvin Versus the Westminster Confession* (Richmond: John Knox Press, 1972), 23. For Calvin, it was a state of pure grace. For the Puritans, however, it was a state of natural independence, since God had created individuals as independent perfect beings. It was only after the Fall that humanity became dependent upon God's grace. Hence, for Rolston, the notion of a prelapsarian covenant of works is foreign to Calvin. He writes, "Of this Calvin knew nothing, for these theological innovations were the work of his successors." For the opposite view, see Lillback, *Binding of God*, 297-304. Admittedly, it is difficult to argue that Calvin held to a prelapsarian covenant of works as articulated in the *WCF*; however, it is equally difficult to argue that such a covenant is antithetical to his teaching. Though he never uses the phrase, he clearly points to the same obligations that came to be known as the covenant of works.

10. Calvin, *Institutes*, II.XII.3.

Evidently, Calvin believes that Adam's disobedience is reckoned to all people. It is not a stretch to deduce, therefore, that if everyone is guilty of disobeying God's command to Adam, then everyone is bound to obey that same command. From this simple deduction, the Westminster divines arrive at the covenant of works.

In support, they appeal to Romans 5:12-20.[11] In verse 12, Paul explains that Adam's sin impacted his descendents: "Wherefore, as by one man sin entered into the world, and death by sin; and so death passed upon all men, for that all have sinned." This means that Adam was our representative in the Garden. As such, he acted on our behalf. When he disobeyed, God reckoned his disobedience to us. As Thomas Watson[12] explains, "Adam being a representative person, while he stood, we stood; when he fell, we fell. We sinned in Adam; so it is in the text, 'In whom all have sinned.'"[13]

It is important to note that Paul initiates a comparison in verse 12 with the word "as." He completes this comparison in verses 18-19, stating, "Therefore as by the offence of one judgment came upon all men to condemnation; even so by the righteousness of one the free gift came upon all men unto justification of life. For as by one man's disobedience many were made sinners, so by the obedience of one shall many be made righteous." For the Westminster divines, these verses imply that, when it comes to humanity, there are two federal heads or representatives. The first is Adam. He is the head of all his posterity: the old humanity. Through his one transgression, there resulted condemnation to all men. This

---

11. For Flavel's treatment of these verses, see *Works*, II:25,117, III:514, V:142, VI:167,171-72.

12. Thomas Watson (d. 1686) was educated at Emmanuel College, Cambridge. He was Presbyterian, and was ejected from the Church of England for Nonconformity in 1662.

13. Thomas Watson, *A Body of Divinity Contained in Sermons Upon the Westminster Assembly's Catechism* (1692; rpt., London: Banner of Truth, 1958), 101.

means that God reckons or imputes Adam's disobedience to all his descendents. Simply put, his sin is their sin, his guilt is their guilt, and his condemnation is their condemnation. The second federal head is Christ. He is the head of all His posterity: the new humanity. Through His one act of righteousness, there resulted justification of life to all men. This means that God reckons or imputes Christ's obedience to all His descendents. Thus, His righteousness becomes their righteousness.

God reckons Adam's "disobedience" and Christ's "obedience" to their respective posterity by way of covenant. God established the covenant of works with Adam. According to the *WCF*, it refers to the life that "was promised to Adam, and in him to his posterity, upon condition of perfect and personal obedience."[14] In failing to keep that covenant, Adam brought condemnation upon himself and his descendents. Everyone has broken that covenant in him. Therefore, everyone is under the curse: death. But there is another covenant: the covenant of grace wherein God "freely offered unto sinners life and salvation by Jesus Christ, requiring of them faith in him that they may be saved, and promising to give unto all those that are ordained unto life his Holy Spirit, to make them willing and able to believe."[15] In short, those who believe in Christ are no longer in Adam (under the covenant of works), because they have been united with Christ (under the covenant of grace), who has fulfilled the covenant of works on their behalf.

The Covenant Theology of John Flavel

Flavel agrees with the Westminster divines,[16] writing, "Christ and Adam are compared as the two roots or common heads of

---

14. *WCF*, VII:II.

15. *WCF*, VII:III.

16. Flavel's adherence to the *WCF* is made evident in his treatise, *An Exposition of the Assembly's Catechism*, *Works*, VI:138-317. In one place, he states, "As chymists extract the spirits of herbs and minerals

mankind, both agreeing in this property of communicating their conditions to those that are theirs."[17] They communicate their conditions under respective covenants: "As there never were, are, or can be more than two common heads appointed by God, namely, *Adam* and *Christ* (1 Cor. 15:45-48; Rom. 5:15-19), so it is impossible there should be more than two covenants, under which mankind stands, under these two common heads."[18] He is referring of course to the covenant of works and the covenant of grace.[19]

What is notable in Flavel's work is that he builds on the *WCF*. In his system of thought, there is a third covenant: the covenant of redemption.[20] He explains this covenant by way of six details.[21] First, it is a "transaction" between "God the Father and God the Son; the former as Creditor, and the latter as a Surety. The Father stands upon satisfaction, the Son engages to give it." Second, the "business" of the transaction is "the redemption and recovery of all God's elect." Third, the "manner" of the transaction is "by mutual engagements

---

into some rare elixir, so have our venerable assembly (lately sitting at Westminster, now in glory) composed for us the most judicious and compendious system, that ever blessed this age" (*Works*, VI:571).

17. Flavel, *Works*, I:189; also see I:491.

18. Flavel, *Works*, III:514; also see VI:69.

19. Flavel, *Works*, VI:166-67,176-77.

20. Flavel, *Works*, I:53; also see IV:114. Flavel's treatise, *The Fountain of Life: A Display of Christ in His Essential and Mediatorial Glory*, consists of 42 sermons. The third sermon is entitled: "The Covenant of Redemption between the Father and the Redeemer," *Works*, I:52-61. It sets the foundation for the remaining sermons, thereby confirming the centrality of this covenant to his thinking. In this respect, he approximates the thinking of John Owen. See *The Works of John Owen*, ed. W.H. Gould (London: Johnstone & Hunter, 1850; rpt., Edinburgh: Banner of Truth, 1977), XII:496-508. For a synopsis of Owen's position, see Steve Griffiths, *Redeem the Time: Sin in the Writings of John Owen* (Fearn: Christian Focus Publications, 2001), 18-29; and Sinclair Ferguson, *John Owen on the Christian Life* (Edinburgh: Banner of Truth Trust, 1987), 20-31.

21. Flavel, *Works*, I:54-58.

and stipulations, each person undertaking to perform his part in order to our recovery." Fourth, the "articles" of the transaction are mutual: the Father promising to do His part by anointing, strengthening, accepting, and rewarding His Son for His work; and the Son promising to do His part by consenting "to be made flesh, to divest, as it were, himself of his glory, to come under the obedience and malediction of the law, and not to refuse any, the hardest sufferings it should please his Father to inflict on him." Fifth, the "performance" of the transaction is "precise" and "punctual," meaning that both the Father and Son fulfill their respective articles. Sixth, the "time" of the transaction is "from eternity."

Conclusion

For Flavel, this covenant of redemption is of paramount importance, because it guarantees the fulfillment of the covenant of grace. In eternity, the Father and Son enter into a covenant to save the elect. In time, the Son becomes a man to accomplish its stipulations. He does so by fulfilling the covenant of works, removing the curse through His death, and ascending to the Father's right hand. From there, He sends forth the Holy Spirit to unite His people to Himself, so that they might partake of the blessings of His humiliation and exaltation. In this way, the covenant of grace is a certainty, resting upon God's eternal purpose for His elect. "Before this world was made," writes Flavel, "then were his delights in us, while as yet we had no existence, but only in the infinite mind and purpose of God, who had decreed this for us in Christ Jesus."[22]

---

22. Flavel, *Works*, I:58.

Chapter 2

---◦◦◦◦---

THE BASIS OF UNION WITH CHRIST

As mentioned in the previous chapter, Flavel sees the salvation of God's people as resting upon the eternal covenant of redemption between God the Father and God the Son. In eternity, the Father and Son enter into a transaction to bring about the salvation of the elect. In time, the Son becomes a man, fulfils the covenant of works, and dies to pay the penalty incurred by His people under that covenant. Having done so, He returns to the Father, from where He sends forth the Holy Spirit to unite His people to Himself. By virtue of that union, they partake of the blessings of the covenant of grace.

In Flavel's mind, therefore, the fulfillment of the covenant of redemption is linked to two great unions.[1] The first is the union of the divine and human natures in Christ; that is known as the "hypostatical" union. The second is the union of Christ and believers by the Holy Spirit; that is known as the "mystical" union. Flavel affirms that the first is the basis for the second.[2] In other words, Christ must become one

---

1. According to Flavel, "There are three illustrious and dazzling unions in scripture: that of three persons in one God, essentially. That of two distinct natures, and persons; by one spirit mystically: and this of two distinct natures in one person, hypostatically" (*Works*, I:75).

2. Flavel, *Works*, IV:129. Joel R. Beeke sees the same approach in Calvin, commenting, "For Calvin, piety is rooted in the believer's mystical union (*unio mystica*) with Christ; thus this union must be our starting point. Such a union is possible because Christ took on our human nature, filling it with his virtue" (*Puritan Reformed Spirituality* [Grand Rapids: Reformation Heritage Books, 2004], 4).

with us hypostatically in order for us to become one with Him mystically.[3]

Because of this emphasis, I will dedicate this chapter to an analysis of Flavel's understanding of the hypostatic union. I am not so much concerned with his thoughts on the mechanics of the incarnation.[4] Suffice it to say, he believes that Christ "took or assumed the true human nature...into the unity of his divine person, with all its integral parts and essential properties; and so was made, or became a true and real man, by that assumption."[5] My interest is in Flavel's understanding of the "grounds and reasons" for this union. In brief, he believes that God the Son became a man "to qualify and prepare him for a full discharge of his mediatorship, in the office of our Prophet, Priest, and King."[6]

Christ as Prophet

For starters, Christ discharges His "mediatorship" as God-man in the office of Prophet. "Had he not this double nature in the unity of his person," writes Flavel, "he could not have

---

3. Edward Pearse speaks of a threefold marriage with Christ. (1) There is the "personal marriage, and that is between the Person of the Son of God, the second Person of the Trinity, and our nature." (2) There is the "mystical marriage, and that is between the Person of Christ, God-man, and the person of believers, as militant here on earth; the whole Christ and the whole believer being made one." (3) There is the "heavenly marriage, and that is between Christ and the Church triumphant above." He adds, "In the first of these lies the foundation of all our happiness; by the second we are brought into an initial participation of it; by the third we are put into the full possession and enjoyment thereof forever" (*The Best Match; or, The Soul's Espousal to Christ* [Morgan: Soli Deo Gloria, 1994], 2-3).

4. Flavel does ponder the "nature" of the hypostatic union in *The Fountain of Life*, dedicating the fifth sermon, "Of Christ's Wonderful Person," to the subject (*Works*, I:72-85). He appropriately refers to Christ's incarnation as "a mystery, by which apprehension is dazzled, invention astonished, and all expression swallowed up" (*Works*, I:74).

5. Flavel, *Works*, I:73.

6. Flavel, *Works*, I:80; also see VI:181-86.

been our Prophet: For, as God, he knows the mind and will of God (John 1:18; 3:13), and as man he is fitted to impart it suitably to us (Deut. 18:15-18; Acts 20:22)."[7] As to the question of how Christ functions as our Prophet, Flavel speaks of "revelation" and "illumination."[8]

Christ's work of "revelation" is external, in that He declares the mind of God to us. He does so in Scripture, which He has given "mediately, by his ministers and officers."[9] He also does so by His incarnation. As John says, "No man hath seen God at any time; the only begotten Son, which is in the bosom of the Father, he hath declared him" (John 1:18).[10] With this verse before him, Flavel asks, "What man can tell the bosom-counsels and secrets of God? Who but he that eternally lay in that bosom can expound them?"[11]

Whereas Christ's work of "revelation" is external, His work of "illumination" is internal. In explaining the need for this internal work, Flavel quotes Edwards Reynolds[12] as

---

7. Flavel, *Works*, I:80.

8. In *The Fountain of Life*, Flavel dedicates one sermon to each. (1) "The First Branch of Christ's Prophetical Office, consisting in the Revelation of the Will of God," *Works*, I:118-30. (2) "The Second Branch of Christ's Prophetical Office, consisting in the Illumination of the Understanding," *Works*, I:131-42. Also see VI:182.

9. Flavel, *Works*, I:123. According to Flavel, Christ's revelation in Scripture has come to us variously, gradually, plainly, powerfully, sweetly, purely, and fully. *Works*, I:123-25.

10. To know the Son is to know the Father: "If ye had known me, ye should have known my Father also" (John 8:19). To believe in the Son is to believe in the Father: "He that believeth on me, believeth not on me, but on him that sent me" (John 12:44). To receive the Son is to receive the Father: "He that receiveth me receiveth him that sent me" (John 13:20). To see the Son is to see the Father: "He that hath seen me hath seen the Father" (John 14:9). To hate the Son is to hate the Father: "He that hateth me hateth my Father also" (John 15:23).

11. Flavel, *Works*, I:122.

12. Edward Reynolds (1599-1676) was a graduate of Oxford, and a member of the Westminster Assembly. He conformed at the time of the Restoration, and became Bishop of Norwich.

follows: "It suffices not that the object be revealed, nor yet that man, the subject of that knowledge, have a due use of his own reason; but it is further necessary that the grace and special assistance of the Holy Spirit be superadded, to open and mollify the heart, and so give it a due taste and relish of the sweetness of spiritual truth."[13] In a word, illumination is necessary, because we are insensible to spiritual truth. This condition is confirmed by Paul, who writes, "But the natural man receiveth not the things of the Spirit of God: for they are foolishness unto him: neither can he know them, because they are spiritually discerned" (1 Cor. 2:14). For this reason, Flavel maintains that Christ must send "forth the Spirit...to carry on this work upon the hearts of his elect."[14] The Holy Spirit does so by enlightening the mind. He becomes a "new light, in which all things appear far otherwise than they did before," "an affecting light...that hath heat and powerful influences," and "a growing light" that causes the soul to grow up "to a greater clearness day by day."[15]

By way of example, these two aspects of Christ's prophetic ministry—"revelation" and "illumination"—are evident in what takes place between Christ and His disciples. First, He reveals the mind of God to them by expounding the Scriptures and informing them: "All things must be fulfilled, which were written in the law of Moses, and in the prophets, and in the psalms, concerning me." Second, He illuminates them by opening "their understanding, that they might understand the scriptures" (Luke 24:44-45).

Christ as Priest

Christ also discharges His "mediatorship" as God-man in the office of Priest. "As Priest, had he not been man, he could have shed no blood; and if not God, it had been no adequate

---

13. Flavel, *Works*, I:133.

14. Flavel, *Works*, I:137.

15. Flavel, *Works*, I:137.

value for us (Heb. 2:17)."[16] When it comes to explaining how Christ ministers as our Priest, Flavel again turns to Edward Reynolds, who writes, "This priesthood of Christ is that function, wherein he comes before God, in our name and place, to fulfill the law, and offer up himself to him a sacrifice of reconciliation for our sins; and by his intercession to continue and apply the purchase of his blood to them for whom he shed it."[17] From this, Flavel affirms that Christ's priesthood consists of two "parts": oblation and intercession. Significantly, these correspond to the high priest's "double office" under the Mosaic Covenant whereby he offered the blood of the sacrifice outside the Holy Place (oblation) and presented the blood of the sacrifice inside the Holy Place (intercession).[18]

Christ's Oblation

In simple terms, Christ's "oblation" is His sacrifice. Flavel sums up the significance of this sacrifice in five details. (1) The "priest" that offers the sacrifice is "Jesus Christ, God-man." This is important, because the "dignity" of His person gives an "inestimable worth" to His offering.[19] (2) The "sacrifice" that Christ offers is His "own blood."[20] According to Flavel, Christ's blood is "invaluably precious," because it is the "blood of the Son of God."[21] It is also "complete and all-sufficient," because its virtue "reacheth backward as far as Adam, and reacheth forward to the last person of the elect." In addition, His blood is "highly pleasing and delightful" in God's sight, because it satisfies His offended justice. (3) The "per-

---

16. Flavel, *Works*, I:80.

17. Flavel, *Works*, I:146-47.

18. In *The Fountain of Life*, Flavel dedicates one sermon to each. (1) "The Excellency of our High Priest's Oblation, being the First Act or Part of His Priestly Office," *Works*, I:154-64. (2) "The Intercession of Christ our High Priest, being the Second Act or Part of His Priestly Office," *Works*, I:165-75. Also see VI:183-85.

19. Flavel, *Works*, I:155.

20. Flavel, *Works*, I:156.

21. See 1 Peter 1:18-19.

son" to whom Christ offers His sacrifice is "God." God must
be appeased, because He is "infinitely wronged, and incensed
by sin."[22] Flavel makes it clear that Christ, with His sacrifice,
approaches this "incensed Majesty...as to a devouring fire."
(4) The "persons" for whom Christ offers His sacrifice are
"God's elect."[23] Christ gives His life for "the sheep,"[24] "the
church of God,"[25] and "the children of God."[26] In short, He

---

22. Flavel, *Works*, I:159.

23. Flavel, *Works*, I:159. He appears to agree with the scholastic
distinction between the "sufficiency" and "efficacy" of Christ's atonement, commenting, "It is confessed, there is sufficiency of virtue in
this sacrifice to redeem the whole world...*but* the efficacy and saving
virtue of this all-sufficient sacrifice, is co-extended with God's election,
so that they all, and no others can, or shall reap the special benefits of
it" (*Works*, I:159-60; also see I:64, 190). According to Robert Kendall,
Calvin did not hold to the doctrine of limited atonement. He affirms
that Theodore Beza is responsible for its introduction into English
Reformed theology (*Calvin and English Calvinism*, 19-20, 25, 29, 76).
For the various views, see Roger Nicole, "John Calvin's View of the
Extent of the Atonement," *Westminster Theological Journal* 47 (1985):
197-225; M. Charles Bell, "Calvin and the Extent of the Atonement,"
Evangelical Quarterly 55 (1983): 115-23; Hans Boersma, "Calvin and the
Extent of the Atonement," *Evangelical Quarterly* 64 (1992): 333-55; W.
Robert Godfrey, "Reformed Thought on the Extent of the Atonement
to 1618," *Westminster Theological Journal* 37 (1975): 133-71; Stephen
Strehle, "The Extent of the Atonement and the Synod of Dort," *Westminster Theological Journal* 51 (1989): 1-23; and G. Michael Thomas,
*The Extent of the Atonement: A Dilemma for Reformed Theology from Cal-
vin to the Consensus (1536-1675)* (Bletchley: Paternoster, 1997). The
most thorough Puritan exposition of the subject is Owen's *The Death
of Death in the Death of Christ, Works*, X:139-479. He argues that Christ's
death procured salvation for His people. This does not limit the value
of His sacrifice, which is infinite. It is more than sufficient for the
salvation of every person because of the greatness of His person and
suffering. However, its efficacy is not determined by its sufficiency,
but by God's purpose.

24. See John 10:15.

25. See Acts 20:28.

26. See John 11:50-52.

takes the place of His people. (5) The "end" for which Christ offers His sacrifice is "reconciliation." Christ's oblation is offered to "atone, pacify, and reconcile God, by giving him a full and adequate compensation or satisfaction for the sins of these his elect."[27] At the cross, Christ satisfies God's justice, thereby appeasing God's wrath and securing God's mercy. He delivers His people from sin by being made sin, and from the curse by being made a curse. As a result, they "have peace with God through our Lord Jesus Christ."[28]

Christ's Intercession

The second "part" of Christ's priesthood is His "intercession." For Flavel, this is "the virtual continuation of his offering once made on earth."[29] Christ "acted the first part on earth, in a state of deep abasement...but he acts this in glory, whereto he is taken up, that he may fulfill his design in dying, and give the work of our salvation its last completing act."[30] In heaven, Christ presents: (1) Himself before God "in our names, and upon our account"; (2) "his blood, and all his sufferings to God, as a moving plea on our account"; and (3) "the prayers of his saints to God, with his merits; and desires that they may for his sake be granted."[31] In this way, He guarantees the application of all that He procured by His crucifixion and resurrection. As Paul declares, "Who shall lay any thing to the charge of God's elect? It is God that justifieth. Who is he that condemneth? It is Christ that died, yea rather, that is risen again, who is even at the right hand of God, who also maketh intercession for us" (Rom. 8:33-34; also see Heb. 7:25).

---

27. Flavel, *Works*, I:160.
28. Rom. 5:1. Flavel, *Works*, I:474-77.
29. Flavel, *Works*, I:165.
30. Flavel, *Works*, I:166.
31. Flavel, *Works*, I:168-69.

The Result of Christ's Priesthood

The first result of Christ's "oblation" and "intercession" is "satisfaction."[32] According to Flavel, "satisfaction is the act of Christ, God-man, presenting himself as our surety in obedience to God and love to us; to do and to suffer all that the law required of us: thereby freeing us from the wrath and curse due to us for sins."[33] When he says that Christ presents Himself "to do and to suffer all that the law required of us," Flavel is referring to Christ's active and passive obedience. (1) By His active obedience, Christ has fulfilled what God requires of us in the Law: obedience. Christ lived as our substitute, rendering perfect obedience to God. (2) By His passive obedience, Christ has fulfilled what God requires of us for breaking the Law: death. Christ died as our substitute, becoming a curse for us. "This twofold obedience," says Flavel, "stands opposed to a twofold obligation that fallen man is under; the one to do what God requires, the other to suffer what he hath threatened for disobedience."[34] By His obedience, therefore, Christ has satisfied God and freed us "from the wrath and curse due to us for sins."

The second result of Christ's priestly work is "acquisition."[35] Flavel remarks, "We lost our inheritance by the fall of Adam; we receive it…by the death of Christ."[36] It includes "all temporal good things," "all spiritual good things," and "all eternal good things."[37] It is summed up in the fact that we are "heirs of God, and joint heirs with Christ" (Rom.

---

32. See Flavel's sermon "A Vindication of the Satisfaction of Christ, as the First Effect or Fruit of His Priesthood" in *The Fountain of Life*, *Works*, I:176-87.

33. Flavel, *Works*, I:179.

34. Flavel, *Works*, I:181.

35. See Flavel's sermon "The Blessed Inheritance Purchased by the Oblation of Christ, being the Second Effect or Fruit of His Priesthood" in *The Fountain of Life*, *Works*, I:188-97.

36. Flavel, *Works*, I:188.

37. Flavel, *Works*, I:191-94.

8:17). This is a central biblical motif, extending back to the Abrahamic Covenant, in which God declares, "And I will establish my covenant between me and thee and thy seed after thee in their generations for an everlasting covenant, to be a God unto thee, and to thy seed after thee" (Gen. 17:7). Paul interprets the fulfillment of that promise as follows: "For ye are the temple of the living God; as God hath said, I will dwell in them, and walk in them; and I will be their God, and they shall be my people" (2 Cor. 6:16). By His "oblation" and "intercession," therefore, Christ has brought us into our inheritance.[38]

Christ as King

Finally, Christ discharges His "mediatorship" as God-man in the office of King. Again, Flavel reminds us of the importance of Christ's two natures to the fulfillment of this office, stating, "As King, had he not been man, he had been an heterogeneous, and so no fit head for us. And if not God, he could neither rule nor defend his body the Church."[39] As for the nature of Christ's kingly office, Flavel believes that it consists in "first subduing the souls of his elect to his spiritual government; then ruling them as his subjects, and ordering all things in the kingdom of Providence for their good."[40]

Flavel develops the significance of Christ's "spiritual government" under three themes. First, he explains how Christ obtains the throne in the heart of His people. "The house," he says, "is conveyed to Christ by him that built it, but the strong man armed keeps the possession of it, till a stronger

---

38. Flavel, *Works*, VI:176.

39. Flavel, *Works*, I:80.

40. Flavel, *Works*, I:199. Here, Flavel identifies two ways in which Christ fulfills His role as our King: spiritually and providentially. In *The Fountain of Life*, he dedicates one sermon to each. (1) "The Kingly Office of Christ, as it is Executed Spiritually upon the Souls of the Redeemed," *Works*, I:198-210. (2) "The Kingly Office of Christ, as it is Executed Providentially in the World for the Redeemed," *Works*, I:211-22. Also see VI:185-86.

than he comes and ejects him (Luke 11:20-22). Christ must fight his way into the soul, though he have a right to enter, as into his dearly purchased possession." Christ wages this war by causing "armies of convictions" to trouble them.[41] In this condition, they look away from themselves for help. Christ draws near, and "hangs forth the white flag of mercy before the soul, giving it hopes it shall be spared, pitied, and pardoned...if yet it will yield itself to Christ." In response, they bring "Christ the keys of all the rooms in the soul." "And thus," says Flavel, "the soul is won to Christ."[42]

Second, Flavel considers how Christ rules His people once He has obtained the throne. In brief, Christ "imposes a new law upon them, and enjoins them to be severe and punctual in their obedience to it"; He "rebukes and chastises souls for the violations and transgressions of his law"; He "restrains and keeps back his servants from iniquity, and withholds them from those courses which their own hearts would incline, and lead them to"; He "protects them in his ways, and suffers them not to relapse from him into a state of sin, and bondage to Satan any more"; He "rewards their obedience, and encourages their sincere service"; and He "pacifies all inward troubles, and commands peace when their spirits are tumultuous."[43]

Third, Flavel identifies the privileges that belong to those who are ruled by Christ: they are "certainly and fully set free from the curse of the Law"; they are released from the "dominion of sin"; they are protected in "all the troubles and dangers to which their souls and bodies are exposed"; they are confident that Christ tenderly bears "their burdens and infirmities"; they enjoy "sweet peace and tranquility of soul"; and they possess "everlasting salvation."[44]

---

41. See Acts 2:37.
42. Flavel, *Works*, I:201-03.
43. Flavel, *Works*, I:203-05.
44. Flavel, *Works*, I:206-07.

Conclusion

As is evident from the foregoing discussion, Christ's three-fold office is essential to our salvation. As Prophet, He reveals God to us. As Priest, He reconciles us to God. As King, He rules over us. "Salvation," says Flavel, "is revealed by Christ as a Prophet, procured by him as a Priest, applied by him as a King. In vain it is revealed, if not purchased; in vain revealed and purchased, if not applied."[45] Again, he comments:

> Had he not, as our Prophet, opened the way of life and salvation to the children of men, they could never have known it; and if they had clearly known it, except, as their Priest, he had offered up himself, to impetrate and obtain redemption for them, they could not have been redeemed virtually by his blood; and if they had been so redeemed, yet had he not lived in the capacity of a King, to apply this purchase of his blood to them, they could have had no actual, personal benefit by his death; for what he revealed as a Prophet, he purchased as a Priest; and what he so revealed and purchased as a Prophet and Priest, he applies as a King.[46]

We began this chapter by observing that, for Flavel, Christ must become one with us hypostatically in order for us to become one with Him mystically. The reason why is now evident: namely, Christ must discharge His "mediatorship" as God-man in His threefold office of Prophet, Priest, and King in order to secure the blessings that He lavishes upon all those who are united with Him by the Spirit.

---

45. Flavel, *Works*, I:143.
46. Flavel, *Works*, I:198-99.

Chapter 3

———— ⊶⊷⊶ ————

THE NATURE OF UNION
WITH CHRIST

As stated in the first chapter, Flavel believes that there are three covenants. The first is the covenant of works, which God established with Adam. In failing to keep it, Adam brought condemnation upon himself and his descendents. The second is the covenant of grace, according to which God graciously accepts Christ's perfect obedience on behalf of those who believe in Him. The third is the covenant of redemption between God the Father and God the Son, who transacted in eternity to save the elect by the covenant of grace.

For Flavel, our participation in the covenant of grace depends upon two great unions. The first is the "hypostatical" union, that is, the union of the divine and human natures in Christ. As noted in the last chapter, this union is essential to the successful discharge of Christ's threefold office of Prophet, Priest, and King. The second is the "mystical" union, that is, the union of Christ and believers by the Holy Spirit. According to Flavel, this union is "an intimate conjunction of believers to Christ, by the imparting of his Spirit to them whereby they are enabled to believe and live in him."[1] In the

---

1. Flavel, *Works*, II:37. Flavel is careful to explain that this union is not "physical," or "essential," nor is it merely "mental," "federal," or "moral" (*Works*, II:38). In his treatise, *The Fountain of Life*, he explains how redemption is secured, whereas in his treatise, *The Method of Grace*, he explains how redemption is applied. The second sermon, "The Union of the Believer with Christ: A Principal Part of Effec-

words of Edward Pearse,[2] "It is that spiritual conjunction or relation that is between Christ and believers, between the person of Christ and the person of believers, arising from his inhabitation in them by his Spirit and their closing with him by faith."[3] Similarly, Joseph Hall[4] describes it as a union "whereby the person of the believer is indissolubly united to the glorious person of the Son of God."[5]

These definitions are based in large part upon 1 Corinthians 12:13, where Paul declares, "For by one Spirit are we all baptized into one body." In other words, the Holy Spirit makes us one with Christ by virtue of His dwelling in us.[6] Flavel describes this union by way of ten marks. (1) It is intimate: "Husband and wife are not so near, soul and body are not so near, as Christ and the believing soul are near to each other." (2) It is supernatural: "We can no more unite ourselves to Christ, than a branch can incorporate itself into another stock." (3) It is immediate: "Every member, the smallest as well as the greatest, hath an immediate condi-

---

tual Application," is dedicated to the nature of our union with Christ (*Works*, II:33-48).

2. Edward Pearse (d. 1673) was a pastor at St. Margaret's, Westminster.

3. Pearse, *Best Match*, 4.

4. Joseph Hall (1574-1656) was a graduate of Cambridge. He became Bishop of Norwich. While Episcopalian in conviction, his theology and spirituality were decidedly "Puritan."

5. Joseph Hall, *Christ Mystical; or, The Blessed Union of Christ and His Members* (London: Hodder and Stoughton, 1893), 36.

6. It is imperative to observe the difference between the Puritan concept of "union with Christ" and what is normally called "mysticism." As Richard Lovelace notes, "Medieval mysticism shares with Platonic mysticism a common structure: that of a threefold path to God, consisting of purification, contemplation, and final union" ("The Anatomy of Puritan Piety: English Puritan Devotional Literature, 1600-1640" in *Christian Spirituality III*, eds. L. Dupré and D. E. Saliers [New York: Crossroad Publishing, 1989], 318). The Puritans, on the other hand, begin with union and stress the mortification of sin, not the purification of the senses.

tion with Christ." (4) It is fundamental: "Destroy this union, and with it you destroy all our fruits, privileges, and eternal hopes." (5) It is efficacious: "Through this union the divine power flows into our souls, both to quicken us with the life of Christ, and to conserve and secure that life in us after it is so infused." (6) It is indissoluble: "Death dissolves the dear union betwixt the husband and wife, friend and friend, yea, betwixt soul and body, but not betwixt Christ and the soul, the bands of this union rot not in the grave." (7) It is honorable: "To be a servant of Christ is a dignity transcendent to the highest advancement among men; but to be a member of Christ, how matchless and singular is the glory thereof." (8) It is comfortable: "Whatever troubles, wants, or distresses befall such, in this is abundant relief and support, Christ is mine, and I am his; what may not a good soul make out of that!" (9) It is fruitful: "Christ is a fruitful root, and makes all the branches that live in him so too." (10) It is enriching: "All that Christ hath becomes ours, either by communication to us, or improvement for us."[7]

The first mark is key to our present discussion: union with Christ is "intimate." According to Flavel, the Bible employs four "lively metaphors" to help us grasp the nature of this intimacy. These are drawn from the "book of nature," corresponding to adhesives, agriculture, anatomy, and marriage.[8] Flavel does not have much to say about the first, but he refers to the other three throughout his works.[9]

Graft and Stock

The first is that of graft and stock. Flavel finds it in Romans 6:5, where Paul says, "For if we have been planted together in the likeness of his death, we shall be also in the likeness of his resurrection." Flavel believes that the term "planted"

---

7. Flavel, *Works*, II:39–42.

8. Flavel, *Works*, II:34–35.

9. Flavel, *Works*, II:34; also see II:143.

conveys the idea of a graft being implanted into a stock. When this happens, the stock's sap or juice immediately passes to the graft. Consequently, the graft receives its vitality from the stock.[10] This "conjunction is so close," says Flavel, "that they become one tree."[11] In the same way, believers are implanted into Christ. This is accomplished by the Holy Spirit whose "work in uniting or ingrafting a soul in Christ, is like the cutting off the graff from its native stock...and closing it with the living, when it is thus prepared, and so enabling it... to suck and draw the vital sap."[12] As a result, believers receive life from Christ. Plus, they are conjoined with Him. Flavel remarks, "As the vital sap of the stock coming into the graff, makes it one of the stock...so the coming of Christ's Spirit into the soul, makes it a member of his mystical body."[13] Hall agrees, "The bough and the tree are not more of one piece than we are of one substance with our Saviour."[14]

The same basic idea is conveyed by Christ when He says, "I am the vine, ye are the branches: He that abideth in me, and I in him, the same bringeth forth much fruit: for without me ye can do nothing" (John 15:5). The roots of the vine receive their nourishment from the soil. This nourishment is transferred to the vine. From there, it travels to the branches. As a result, the branches produce fruit. Without that nourishment, the branches would die. Similarly, there is a vital, organic union between Christ and believers. We draw on Christ's life through the Holy Spirit, who dwells in us. As Paul says, "I am crucified with Christ: nevertheless I live; yet not I, but Christ liveth in me: and the life which I now live in the flesh I live by the faith of the Son of God, who loved me, and gave himself for me" (Gal. 2:20).

---

10. Flavel, *Works*, II:144.
11. Flavel, *Works*, V:147.
12. Flavel, *Works*, II:38.
13. Flavel, *Works*, IV:212.
14. Hall, *Christ Mystical*, 57.

Head and Body

The second metaphor is that of head and body as found in Ephesians 4:15-16, where Paul says that we are to "grow up into him in all things, which is the head, even Christ: from whom the whole body fitly joined together and compacted by that which every joint supplieth, according to the effectual working in the measure of every part, maketh increase of the body unto the edifying of itself in love." This metaphor means that believers stand to Christ in the same relation as the members of a physical body stand to their head, and Christ stands to believers in the same relation as the head of a physical body stands to its members.[15] What relation is this? Just as the head gives sense and motion to its physical body, Christ gives sense and motion to His mystical body. Flavel states, "As all the members of the natural body receive animation, sense, and motion, by their union with their natural head; so all believers, the members of Christ, receive spiritual life and animation by their union with Christ their mystical head (Eph. 4:15-16)."[16]

Husband and Wife

The third metaphor is that of husband and wife. In Ephesians 5:30-31, Paul quotes Genesis 2:23-24, where Moses writes, "And Adam said, 'This is now bone of my bones, and flesh of my flesh: she shall be called Woman, because she was taken out of Man.' Therefore shall a man leave his father and his mother, and shall cleave unto his wife: and they shall be one flesh."[17] In these verses, we discover three important features of the relationship between Adam and Eve. (1) Eve is taken out of Adam. She is, therefore, flesh of his flesh and bone of his bones. This is important, because it shows that

---

15. According to Flavel, Christ is head by way of "influence," "government," "consultation," and "honour" (*Works*, II:45).

16. Flavel, *Works*, II:426.

17. For Flavel's comments on these verses, see *Works*, I:450, II:35, IV:212.

Eve's existence is derived from Adam. (2) Eve is brought to Adam. They are joined together, in that they cleave to one another, thereby becoming one flesh. (3) Eve completes Adam. Prior to God's creation of Eve, there was no suitable "help meet" for Adam (Gen. 2:20). But once God created Eve, Adam was complete.

There are invaluable lessons here concerning the marriage relationship. That, however, is not Paul's primary concern. He says, "This is a great mystery: but I speak concerning Christ and the church" (Eph. 5:32). This means that the union between Adam and Eve typifies the union between Christ and the church. How? (1) As Eve is taken out of Adam, so too the church is taken out of Christ. When Christ died, the soldier pierced His side with a spear. Water and blood flowed from that wound, the purchasing price for the church. The church is, therefore, flesh of His flesh and bone of His bones. Hall comments, "Oh, happy conjunction of the second Adam with her which was taken out if his most precious side! Oh, heavenly and complete marriage!"[18] (2) As Eve is brought to Adam, so too the church is brought to Christ. They are joined together, becoming one flesh— one body. In the words of Pearse, "Herein lies the very soul and substance of this spiritual marriage, in a spiritual union between Christ and the believer. Though Christ and the soul were two before, two who were strangers to each other, yet in this marriage or espousal they become one, and so much one that all the world can never make them two again, can never dissolve this union."[19] (3) As Eve completes Adam, so too the church completes Christ.[20] As Paul puts it, the church is "his body, the fulness of him that filleth all in all" (Eph. 1:23).

---

18. Hall, *Christ Mystical*, 46.

19. Pearse, *Best Match*, 6-7.

20. This does not mean that Christ Himself is "lacking" in anything. As the eternal Son of God, He is perfect and complete. It does mean that, in His "mediatorship," He is incomplete without His people.

Conclusion

Each of these "lively" metaphors—as Flavel calls them—serves to convey the "intimate" nature of the union that exists between Christ and His church. Each in its own way stresses the fact that the church derives its life from Christ. The graft derives its vitality from the stock. The body derives its motion from the head. Eve derives her existence from Adam. Likewise, "All divine and spiritual life," says Flavel, "is originally in the Father, and cometh not to us, but by and through the Son (John 5:26)...but the Son communicates this life which is in him to none but by and through the Spirit (Rom. 8:2).... The Spirit must therefore first take hold of us, before we can live in Christ."[21]

---

21. Flavel, *Works*, II:37.

Chapter 4

--- ⦿ ---

THE ACT OF UNION WITH CHRIST

We concluded the last chapter with these words from Flavel: "The Spirit must therefore first take hold of us, before we can live in Christ."[1] This brings us to the manner in which we are united with Christ. Repeatedly, Flavel stresses the fact that "there are only two ligaments, or bands of union betwixt Christ and the soul, viz. the Spirit on his part, and faith on ours."[2] Likewise, Hall says, "As there are two persons betwixt whom this union is made, Christ and the believer, so each of them concurs to the happy effecting of it: Christ, by his Spirit diffused through the hearts of all the regenerate, giving life and activity to them; the believer, laying hold by faith upon Christ, so working in him; and these do so react upon each other that, from their mutual operation results this gracious union whereof we treat."[3] To sum up, mystical union is the direct result of Christ's taking hold of us by His Spirit, and our taking hold of Christ by our faith.[4]

Christ takes hold of us by His Spirit
In terms of sequence, Christ must take hold of us before we can take hold of Him. He makes that clear when He says, "No man can come to me, except the Father which hath sent me draw him" (John 6:44; see also John 6:65). The reason

---

1. Flavel, *Works*, II:37; also see II:85, VI:191.

2. Flavel, *Works*, II:39.

3. Hall, *Christ Mystical*, 127.

4. Beeke refers to these two as "piety's double bond," and demonstrates their importance to Calvin's understanding of communion with Christ (*Puritan Reformed Spirituality*, 5).

we cannot come to Him is this: our mind is darkened, our affections are hardened, and our will is enslaved. We will return to that predicament in just a moment. For now, suffice it to say, we possess "a free will" that is in bondage to sin.[5] For this reason, God must draw us to Christ.[6] And, according to Flavel, God does so by "powerfully and effectually" inclining our will.[7] This act of "inclining" does not involve "force" or "compulsion."[8] Nor does it involve a "bare proposal."[9] In other words, God does not merely propose Christ to us, and then leave us alone to make a decision. If He did, we would never come to Christ. As Flavel explains:

> The admirers of nature talk much of the sovereignty, virginity, and liberty of the will, as if it alone had escaped the fall, and that no more but a moral suasion is needed to open it to Christ; that is, that God doth need no more to save men than the devil doth to damn them. But if ever God make you sensible what the work of saving conversion is, you will quickly find that your will is lame, its freedom to spiritual things gone; you will cry out of a wounded will, as well as of a dark head, and a hard heart.[10]

In Flavel's system of thought, we are free to choose whatever we want. The problem is this: we never want God. Therefore, we will never choose Him. Paul makes that clear

5. For Flavel's view on Pelagianism, see *Works*, II:506-07.

6. In *The Method of Grace*, Flavel includes eleven sermons that expound the "motives" God uses to draw sinners to Christ. *Works*, II:156-286.

7. Flavel, *Works*, II:68. Flavel considers this subject in two sermons in *The Method of Grace*. (1) "The Work of the Spirit as the internal and most effectual Means of the Application of Christ," *Works*, II:67-83. (2) "The Work of the Spirit by which the Soul is enabled to apply Christ," *Works*, II:84-101.

8. Flavel, *Works*, II:68.

9. Flavel, *Works*, II:70.

10. Flavel, *Works*, IV:51; also see II:423, III:436.

when he says, "there is none that seeketh after God" (Rom. 3:11). For this reason, God must incline us to Himself. When Flavel says that God does so "powerfully and effectually," he is referring to "that which the schools call *gratia efficax*, effectual grace; and others *victrix delectation*, an overcoming, conquering delight." He adds, "The work is carried on with a most efficacious sweetness. So that the liberty of the will is not infringed, whilst the obstinacy of the will is effectually subdued and over-ruled."[11] Flavel's concept of "efficacious sweetness" is appreciated only in the context of his understanding of the soul in humanity's threefold state: creation, degeneration, and regeneration.

Man, by Creation

As created by God, "the soul is the most wonderful and astonishing piece of divine workmanship; it is no hyperbole to call it the breath of God, the beauty of men, the wonder of angels, and the envy of devils. One soul is of more value than all the bodies in the world."[12] But what exactly is it? By way of definition, Flavel says, "The soul of man is a vital, spiritual, and immortal substance, endowed with an understanding, will, and various affections; created with an inclination to the body, and infused thereinto by the Lord."[13] In this definition, Flavel identifies three faculties.[14]

---

11. Flavel, *Works*, II:70; also see IV:92, 211, VI:193-94.

12. Flavel, *Works*, II:495. Most of the insights in this section are taken from *Pneumatologia: A Treatise of the Soul of Man*, in *Works*, II:475-III:238.

13. Flavel, *Works*, II:495.

14. This tripartite division of the soul is a minor alteration of the more common bipartite division within Reformed theology. Calvin states, "The soul consists of two faculties, understanding and will" (*Institutes*, I.XV.7). Calvin does not deny the function of the affections, but prefers to include them under the banner of the will. The will, therefore, has two components: inclination (or affections) and choice. Many of the Puritans, however, designate the affections as a faculty in its own right. Flavel seems to fluctuate between a bi-partite and

The first is the "understanding." This is the "noble lead-ing faculty" of the soul, which distinguishes us from the "brutes."[15] "This faculty," says Flavel, "is by philosophers called το ηγεμονιχον, the leading faculty; because the will follows its practical dictates. It sits at the helm, and guides the course of the soul; not impelling, or rigorously enforcing its dictates upon the will; for the will cannot be so imposed upon; but by giving it a directive light, or pointing, as it were, with its finger, what it ought to chuse, and what to refuse."[16]

---

tri-partite division. In the final analysis, the difference is unimportant, given the fact that the function of the affections remains the same in both paradigms.

15. Flavel, *Works*, II:502.

16. Flavel, *Works*, II:503. Flavel is not suggesting that the will necessarily follows the dictates of the mind. In referring to the mind as the "leading faculty," he means that: (1) the will ought to follow the mind; (2) the knowledge of God always begins in the mind; and (3) the will cannot choose that which is unknown to the mind. This perspective echoes Calvin, who states, "Let the office…of understanding be to distinguish between objects, as each seems worthy of approval or disapproval; while that of the will, to choose and follow what the understanding pronounces good, but to reject and flee what it disapproves" (*Institutes*, I.XV.7). There are two main schools of thought surrounding Calvin's perspective: in-tellectualism and voluntarism. According to Richard Muller, these terms refer to "the two faculties of soul, intellect and will, and to the question of the priority of the one over the other, intellectual-ism indicates a priority of intellect, voluntarism a priority of the will" ("*Fides* and *Cognitio* in Relation to the Problem of Intellect and Will in the Theology of John Calvin," *Calvin Theological Jour-nal* 25 [1990]: 211). As for Calvin's view, Muller writes, "Calvin appears to echo the voluntarist tradition insofar as he places choice in the will and does not make the intellect either efficiently or finally the cause of the will's choice…. Under the terms of Cal-vin's ideal or philosophical definition, reason ought to announce the good and the will follow the dictates of reason, albeit freely and of its own choice" ("*Fides* and *Cognitio*," 215-16). Muller makes an insightful observation when he distinguishes between *temporal* and *causal* priority in Calvin's thought. In this paradigm, the will is

The second faculty is the "will." By it, we choose or refuse "the things which the understanding discerns and knows."[17] According to Flavel, the will possesses two "excellencies." The first is freedom, meaning it cannot be compelled or forced.[18] The second is dominion, meaning it has "absolute" command over the body and "persuasive" command over the passions.[19]

The third faculty is the "affections." In brief, they are the inclination or disinclination of the soul to a particular object. The soul loves that which it perceives to be good. This love is manifested in desire (when the object is absent) and delight (when the object is present). Conversely, the soul hates that which it perceives as evil. This hatred is manifested in fear (when the object is absent) and sorrow (when the object is present).[20] In Flavel's words, the affections are "designed

---

dependent upon the intellect for its object, because the will is unable to choose the unknown. However, dependence is not the same as determination. The Puritans (including Flavel) adopt this view of the temporal priority of the mind.

17. Flavel, *Works*, II:506.

18. Flavel, *Works*, II:506.

19. Flavel, *Works*, II:508.

20. Flavel's concept of the affections is found in Augustine, who identifies four motions of the soul: desire, fear, joy, and sorrow (*The City of God* in *A Select Library of the Nicene and Post-Nicene Fathers of the Christian Church: Vol. II*, ed. P. Schaff [New York: Random House, 1948], XIV:5). Desire and joy are the "volition of consent" to a "loved" object: desire occurs when consent takes the form of seeking the object, and joy occurs when consent takes the form of enjoying it. On the other hand, fear and sorrow are the "volition of aversion" from a "hated" object: fear occurs when aversion takes the form of turning from the object, and sorrow occurs when aversion takes the form of experiencing it (*City of God*, XIV:6). In this paradigm, love and hatred ultimately determine the response of the other affections: desire is yearning for what is loved; joy is delighting in what is loved; fear is fleeing from what is hated; and sorrow is experiencing what is hated. From this, Augustine argues that as long as the object of an individual's love is "well-directed," the affections are good. This changes,

and appointed for the happiness of man, in the promoting and securing its chiefest good, to which purpose they have a natural aptitude."[21] The chiefest good, of course, is God.

In innocence, these three faculties—understanding, will, and affections—functioned properly, meaning Adam knew God with his mind, loved God with his affections, and obeyed God with his will.[22] In contemplating this state, Flavel declares, "What a beautiful and blessed creature was the soul of man at first, whilst it stood in its integrity. His mind was bright, clear, and apprehensive of the law and will of God; his will cheerfully complied therewith.... The law of God was fairly engraven upon the table of his heart. Principles of holiness and righteousness were inlaid in the frame of his mind, fitting him for an exact and punctual discharge of his duties both to God and man."[23]

Man, by Degeneration

At the Fall, however, this "blessed and beautiful creature" was corrupted. "Sin," says Flavel, "hath defaced its beauty, razed out the Divine image which was its glory, and stamped the image of Satan upon it."[24] This "image of Satan" is impressed upon the three faculties of the soul, in that they no

---

of course, if the object of an individual's love is "ill-directed" (*City of God*, XIV:7). Prior to the Fall, the object of Adam's love was God and, as a result, the affections were "good." This condition, however, was terminated at the time of the Fall when love for God was lost and, consequently, the affections became "evil." At regeneration, the individual's love is again "well-directed," and the affections respond accordingly. Augustine summarizes, "The citizens of the holy city of God, who live according to God in the pilgrimage of this life, both fear and desire, and grieve and rejoice. And because their love is rightly placed, all these affections of theirs are right" (*City of God*, XIV:9).

21. Flavel, *Works*, II:509; also see III:158.

22. Flavel, *Works*, V:425. For Flavel, this is the image of God in humanity (*Works*, V:529, VI:163).

23. Flavel, *Works*, II:539.

24. Flavel, *Works*, II:539.

longer function in the manner they were intended: "Where sin is in dominion, the soul is in a very sad condition; for it darkens the understanding, depraves the conscience, stiffens the will, hardens the heart, misplaces and disorders all the affections; and thus every faculty is wounded by the power and dominion of sin over the soul."[25]

In brief, while in a state of degeneration, the will is controlled by an understanding that prefers darkness to light and by affections that prefer evil to good. Consequently, it is in bondage to sin.[26] This means that our will (although free in the actions it performs) is captive in its way of performing them.[27] Because of this "disorder," the sensitive appetite now rules over the rational appetite, meaning we are inclined "to things that are earthly and sensual, relishing more sweetness and delight in them, than in the blessed God."[28]

---

25. Flavel, *Works*, II:192; also see V:426.

26. For an excellent treatment of this subject, see H. J. McSorley, *Luther: Right or Wrong? An Ecumenical-Theological Study of Luther's Major Work, The Bondage of the Will* (New York: Newman Press, 1969).

27. Flavel, *Works*, IV:42-48,196-97. This echoes Calvin, who writes, "For we do not deny that man was created with free choice, endowed as he was with sound intelligence of mind and uprightness of will. We do declare that our choice is now held captive under bondage to sin, but how did this come about except by Adam's misuse of free choice when he had it?" (*The Bondage and Liberation of the Will*, ed. A. N. S. Lane [Grand Rapids: Baker Books, 1996], 47). According to Calvin, people are free to choose whatever they want. The problem is that, because of the Fall, they only want evil. In short, the will is in bondage to sin. He adds, "A bound will, finally, is one which because of its corruptness is held captive under the authority of evil desires, so that it can choose nothing but evil, even if it does so of its own accord and gladly, without being driven by external impulse" (*Bondage and Liberation of the Will*, 69).

28. Flavel, *Works*, VI:53. Flavel sees this occurring in four areas: (1) love of the world; (2) love of ambition; (3) inordinate love of freedom and pleasure; and (4) excessive love of life (*Works*, VI:54-58; also see VI:481).

Man, by Regeneration

But all is not lost. "By regeneration," writes Flavel, "this disordered soul is set right again." In a word, it is "by grace restored and rectified."[29] This renewal begins with "illumination" in the darkened understanding.[30] It proceeds to "tenderness" in the hardened affections,[31] meaning the affections are stirred to hate what they formerly loved (sin) and love what they formerly hated (God).[32] From the affections, renewal proceeds to "subjection" in the enslaved will.[33] In other words, the will becomes subject to Christ.

Flavel's affinity in all this with the Westminster divines is clearly evident. They write:

> All those whom God hath predestinated unto life, and those only, he is pleased, in his appointed and accepted time, effectually to call, by His Word and Spirit, out of that state of sin and death, in which they are by nature, to grace and salvation by Jesus Christ; enlightening their minds, spiritually and savingly, to understand the things of God; taking away their heart of stone, and giving unto them an heart of flesh; renewing their wills, and by his almighty power determining them to that which is good.[34]

---

29. Flavel, *Works*, V:426. For thorough Puritan treatments of regeneration, see Stephen Charnock, *Discourses on Regeneration* in *The Works of Stephen Charnock: Vol. III*, ed. James Nichol (London, 1865; rpt., Edinburgh: Banner of Truth, 1986); and George Swinnock, *The Door of Salvation Opened by the Key of Regeneration; or, A treatise containing the nature, necessity, marks and means of regeneration: as also the duty of the regenerate* in *The Works of George Swinnock: Vol. V*, ed. James Nichol (London, 1868; rpt., Edinburgh: Banner of Truth, 1992).

30. Flavel, *Works*, II:93.

31. Flavel, *Works*, II:93.

32. Flavel, *Works*, II:199.

33. Flavel, *Works*, II:93.

34. *WCF*, X:I.

For Flavel, this is the nature of conversion: "the turning of the whole man to God."[35] He comments, "In all true conversion there is a positive turning unto God, a whole heart-choice of him, for your supreme and ultimate happiness and portion (Ps. 73:25) and of the Lord Jesus Christ, as your Prince and Saviour.... And thus it brings forth the new man, and the whole frame of your heart and life is marvelously changed and altered."[36]

That is how Christ takes hold of us by His Spirit. He draws us "powerfully and effectually," in that He causes our understanding to know Him and our affections to love Him and our will to embrace Him. This is "an overcoming, conquering delight...a most efficacious sweetness," as a result of which we "willingly" come to Christ.

We take hold of Christ by our faith

"Three things," says Flavel, "must be wrought upon man, before he can come to Christ: His blind understanding must be enlightened; his hard and rocky heart must be broken and melted; his stiff, fixed, and obstinate will must be conquered and subdued."[37] The last is "the door of the soul, at which the Spirit of God knocks for entrance. When this is won, the soul is won to Christ."[38] Christ, therefore, sends forth the Holy Spirit to enlighten our minds and soften our hearts. We, in turn, perceive the glory of God in Christ, and willingly embrace Him by faith.[39] And this is the marriage knot that binds us to Him.

---

35. Flavel, *Works*, VI:537.

36. Flavel, *Works*, VI:537.

37. Flavel, *Works*, II:322; also see VI:262-63.

38. Flavel, *Works*, II:509.

39. In *The Method of Grace*, Flavel devotes two sermons to this subject. Both are entitled, "The Excellency of Saving Faith by which we do actually and effectually apply Christ to our own Souls," *Works*, II:102-40. For his discussion of "four opinions" concerning "the interest of faith in our justification," see *Works*, II:118-20. Flavel views faith

Flavel develops his concept of faith by affirming that it includes five ingredients. The first is "knowledge": we must understand the truth concerning Christ as revealed in the gospel. The second is "assent": we must agree with that truth. The third is "approbation": we must esteem Christ as the "most excellent, suitable, and complete remedy for all our wants, sins, and dangers, that ever could be prepared by the wisdom and love of God for us." The fourth is "consent": we must receive Christ. The fifth is "acceptance": we must accept the "terms upon which Christ is tendered to us in the gospel."[40]

From the above, it is again evident that Flavel views faith as engaging the three faculties of the soul. "Knowledge" and "assent" are acts of the understanding. "Approbation" is an act of the affections. "Consent" and "acceptance" are acts of the will. In this way, we see that faith involves the whole man and it is, therefore, the whole man who takes hold of Christ. As Flavel remarks, "To receive all Christ, is to receive his person clothed with all his offices; and to receive him with all you heart, is to receive him into your understanding, will, and affections (Acts 8:37). As there is nothing in Christ that may be refused, so there is nothing in you from which he must be excluded."[41] Similarly, Pearse comments, "To know and apprehend Christ is an act of the mind or understanding, but to choose and embrace Christ is an act of the will

---

as the "instrument" in our justification; "it is the hand that receives the righteousness of Christ that justifies us" (*Works*, II:120).

40. Flavel, *Works*, II:106-10; also see IV:144-46. Pearse speaks of the threefold act of faith. (1) There is "choice or election." "The soul accepts and embraces him; he cleaves to him and fastens upon him, resolving to have none but him alone." (2) There is "trust or dependence." The soul "bottoms upon Christ, anchors upon Christ, rests and relies upon Christ for all life and peace, for all grace on earth and glory in heaven." (3) There is "resignation or subjection." "He gives up himself unto the power and possession of Jesus Christ to be ruled, governed, and saved by him as he sees good" (*Best Match*, 41-48).

41. Flavel, *Works*, VI:140.

and affections. And though faith has its rise and origin in the mind, yet it has its completion and perfection in the will and affections—these liking, choosing, and embracing him, and that in a way suitable to what the mind sees and apprehends concerning him."[42]

Conclusion

My purpose in this chapter was simply to demonstrate that, for Flavel, there are two "bands of union" between Christ and believers: Christ takes hold of us by His Spirit, and we take hold of Christ by our faith. Flavel sums it up best, writing:

> This is the *bond of our union* with Christ; that union is begun in our vivification, and completed in our actual receiving of Christ; the first is the bond of union on the Spirit's part, the second a bond of union on our part. "Christ dwelleth in our hearts by faith" (Eph. 3:17). And therein it is a door opened to let in many rich blessings to the soul; for, by uniting us to Christ, it brings us into special favour and acceptation with God (Eph. 1:6). Makes us the special objects of Christ's conjugal love and delight (Eph. 5:29). Draws from his heart sympathy and a tender sense of all our miseries and burdens (Heb. 4:15).[43]

---

42. Pearse, *Best Match*, 177.
43. Flavel, *Works*, II:116.

Chapter 5

THE BLESSINGS OF UNION WITH CHRIST

We concluded the previous chapter with Flavel's assertion that union with Christ is "a door opened to let in many rich blessings to the soul."[1] In other words, by virtue of the mystical union, believers participate in Christ's spiritual privileges; namely, they have communion with Him in His names, titles, righteousness, holiness, death, resurrection, and glory.[2] In brief, a great transaction takes place. "Thy union with his person," explains Flavel, "brings interest in his properties along with it. Whatever he is, or hath, it is for thee."[3] Pearse agrees, "Behold, whatever Christ is or has, which believers are capable of, is all theirs, and they all hold communion with him therein."[4] For Flavel, the implications of this are summed up in 1 Corinthians 1:30, where Paul declares, "But of him are ye in Christ Jesus, who of God is made unto us wisdom, and righteousness, and sanctification, and redemp-

---

1. Flavel, *Works*, II:116.

2. Flavel, *Works*, II:145-48.

3. Flavel, *Works*, VI:80; also see II:144. Similarly, Calvin writes, "But since Christ has been so imparted to you with all his benefits that all his things are made yours, that you are made a member of him, indeed one with him, his righteousness overwhelms your sins; his salvation wipes out your condemnation; with his worthiness he intercedes that your unworthiness may not come before God's sight" (*Institutes*, III.II.24).

4. Pearse, *Best Match*, 10.

tion."[5] Here, Paul identifies four blessings (or privileges) that flow from Christ to all those who are one with Him.

Christ has become to us wisdom

The first is "wisdom." We stand in need of wisdom, because we are foolish by nature. As Paul says, "There is none that understandeth"(Rom. 3:11). With this verse in view, Flavel remarks, "Lapsed man is not only deep in misery, but grossly ignorant, both that he is so, and how to recover himself from it: Sin hath left him at once senseless of his state, and at a perfect loss about the true remedy."[6] In a word, we are spiritually blind. And as blind men are insensible to the strongest rays of light, we too are insensible to the strongest rays of God's glory.

But Paul says, "of him are ye in Christ Jesus, who of God is made unto us wisdom." According to Flavel, Christ becomes to us wisdom in two ways.[7] First, He improves "those treasures of wisdom that are in himself, for the benefit of such souls as are united to him." Second, He imparts "his wisdom to them by the Spirit of illumination." Similarly, Hall speaks of the imputation and impartation of Christ's wisdom:

> Neither is Christ made our wisdom only in respect of heavenly wisdom imparted to us, but in respect of his perfect wisdom imputed unto us. Alas, our ignorances and sinful misprisions are many and great; where should we appear if our faith did not fetch succour from our all-wise and all-sufficient Mediator? O Saviour, we are wise in Thee, our Head, how weak soever we are of ourselves. Thine infinite wisdom and goodness both

---

5. In *The Method of Grace*, Flavel devotes his first sermon to this verse. It is entitled, "The general Nature of the effectual Application of Redemption stated," *Works*, II:15-32. For Hall's treatment of this verse, see *Christ Mystical*, 96-117.

6. Flavel, *Works*, II:16.

7. Flavel, *Works*, II:16.

covers and makes up all our defects. The wife cannot be poor while the husband is rich.[8]

The basis for Christ becoming to us "wisdom" is the hypostatic union. We need a prophet to reveal God to us. We also need a prophet to dispel the darkness that pervades our minds. As the God-man, Christ is that Prophet. When we become one with Him mystically, we partake of the benefits of His prophetic office. Simply put, He imparts the knowledge of God to us, and enables us to receive it.

Christ has become to us righteousness
The second blessing is "righteousness." We stand in need of righteousness, because we are unrighteous by nature. Paul declares, "There is none righteous, no, not one" (Rom. 3:10). God gave a commandment to Adam as our federal head. When Adam disobeyed, we disobeyed. His sin is our sin, and his unrighteousness is our unrighteousness.[9] At Sinai, God gave the Law. It is summed up in two commandments: "Thou shalt love the Lord thy God with all thy heart, and with all thy soul, and with all thy mind.... Thou shalt love thy neighbour as thyself" (Matt. 22:36-40). We fail to love like this; consequently, all our words, deeds, and thoughts are unrighteous in God's sight.

But Paul says, "By him are ye in Christ Jesus, who of God is made unto us...righteousness" (1 Cor. 1:30). This is, of course, a reference to justification. According to the *WCF*, God justifies sinners "by imputing the obedience and satisfaction of Christ unto them, they receiving and resting on him and his righteousness by faith; which faith they have not of themselves, it is the gift of God."[10] Flavel agrees, affirming that justification consists of two parts.[11] (1) There is

8. Hall, *Christ Mystical*, 99-100.
9. See Rom. 5:12-19.
10. *WCF*, XI:I.
11. Flavel, *Works*, VI:196-97.

the pardon of sin. When God justifies us, He charges our sin to Christ.[12] Christ died as our substitute, bearing the curse of the Law. Because our sin is charged to Christ, God forgives us. (2) There is the acceptance of our persons as righteous. When God justifies us, He credits Christ's righteousness to us. Christ lived as our substitute, fulfilling the requirements of the Law. Because Christ's righteousness is credited to us, God declares us to be righteous. As Flavel states, "Christ is made of God unto us *righteousness*, complete and perfect righteousness, whereby our obligation to punishment is dissolved, and thereby a solid foundation for a well-settled peace of conscience is firmly established."[13]

The basis for Christ becoming to us "righteousness" is once again the hypostatic union. We need a priest to mediate between God and us by removing our condemnation and giving us what we lack: righteousness. As the God-man, Christ is that priest. When we become one with Him mystically, we partake of the benefits of His priestly office. What is ours becomes His; God reckons our sin to Christ. What is His becomes ours; God reckons Christ's righteousness to us. As Hall declares, "What a marvelous and happy exchange is here! We are nothing but sin: Christ is perfect righteousness. He is made our sin that we might be made his righteousness."[14]

Christ has become to us sanctification

The third blessing is "sanctification." According to Flavel, this "is the most precious thing in the world, it is the image of God."[15] We stand in need of it, because we are unholy by nature. As seen in the previous chapter, sin has corrupted the faculties of the soul. The understanding is darkened, the affections are hardened, and the will is enslaved. Flavel says

---

12. See 2 Cor. 5:21.

13. Flavel, *Works*, II:16; also see II:36.

14. Hall, *Christ Mystical*, 101.

15. Flavel, *Works*, II:147.

that sin has "defaced" the soul's beauty, and "razed out the Divine image which was its glory, and stamped the image of Satan upon it."[16] Therefore, David's cry is true of us all: "Behold, I was shapen in iniquity; and in sin did my mother conceive me" (Ps. 51:5).[17]

But Paul says, "of him are ye in Christ Jesus, who of God is made unto us…sanctification" (1 Cor. 1:30). This means that Christ relieves "us against the dominion and pollutions of our corruptions."[18] Paul asserts in Romans 6:6 that our old man is crucified with Christ. The purpose of this crucifixion is that "the body of sin might be destroyed." Paul develops the consequences of this, asking, "Know ye not, that to whom ye yield yourselves servants to obey, his servants ye are to whom ye obey; whether of sin unto death, or of obedience unto righteousness?" (Rom. 6:16). According to this verse, there are two masters: sin, resulting in death; and righteousness, resulting in life.[19] The first master rules over those in Adam, whereas the second rules over those in Christ. Believers are united with Christ and, therefore, are no longer in Adam. This union means that they are freed from sin and enslaved to righteousness.

This is central to Flavel's mindset as it implies that the old life of sin in Adam is past. Believers are brought from that old life, the end of which was death, into a new life, the end of which is righteousness. He says, "In Christ dwells the fullness of grace, and from him, our head, it is derived and communicated to us; thus he that sanctifieth, and they that are sanctified, are all of one (Heb. 2:11)."[20] Again:

> What was done upon the person of Christ, was not only virtually done upon us, considered in him as a

---

16. Flavel, *Works*, II:539.

17. Flavel, *Works*, II:76, 321.

18. Flavel, *Works*, II:17.

19. See Rom. 6:13-20.

20. Flavel, *Works*, II:147.

common public representative person, in which sense, we are said to die with him, and live with him, to be crucified with him, and buried with him, but it was also intended for a platform, or idea, of what is to be done by the Spirit, actually upon our souls and bodies, in our single persons. As he died for sin, so the Spirit applying his death to us in the work of mortification, causes us to die to sin, by the virtue of his death: And as he was quickened by the Spirit, and raised unto life, so the Spirit applying unto us the life of Christ, causeth us to live, by spiritual vivification.[21]

As in the case of "wisdom" and "righteousness," the basis for Christ becoming to us "sanctification" is the hypostatic union. We need a king to break the power of sin over us. As the God-man, Christ is that king. He is stronger than the "strong man" that binds us (Luke 11:21-22). He is invested with all power and authority in heaven and on earth. When we become one with Him mystically, we partake of the benefits of His kingly office. He subdues our will, bringing it into line with God's will. Walter Marshall[22] puts it like this: "If we be joined to Christ, our hearts will be no longer left under the power of sinful inclinations, or in a mere indifference of inclination to good or evil; but they will be powerfully endowed with a power, bent, and propensity to the practice of holiness, by the Spirit of Christ dwelling in us, and inclining us to mind spiritual things and to lust against the flesh (Rom. 8:1, 4-5; Gal. 5:17)."[23]

---

21. Flavel, *Works*, II:18-19.

22. Walter Marshall (1628-1680) was a graduate of Oxford. He ministered at Hursley in Hampshire, but was ejected from the Church of England for Nonconformity in 1662.

23. Walter Marshall, *The Gospel Mystery of Sanctification* (1670; Grand Rapids: Reformation Heritage Books, 1999), 37. This is an excellent exposition of the Puritan doctrine of sanctification.

Christ has become to us redemption

The fourth blessing is "redemption." Wisdom, righteousness, and sanctification are tremendous privileges; nevertheless, says Flavel, "Something is required beyond all this to make our happiness perfect and entire, wanting nothing; and that is the removal of those doleful effects and consequences of sin, which...still lie upon the souls and bodies of illuminated, justified, and sanctified persons."[24] By "doleful effects and consequences of sin," he means those "swarms of vanity, loads of deadness, and fits of unbelief" that assail the soul, plus those "many diseases, deformities, and pains" that oppress the body. Hall agrees, "Those who in this life are enlightened by his wisdom, justified by his merits, sanctified by his grace are yet conflicting with manifold temptations and dangers, till, upon their happy death and glorious resurrection, they shall be fully freed by their ever-blessed and victorious Redeemer."[25] This implies that we still struggle with the presence of sin.

But Paul says, "By him are ye in Christ Jesus, who of God is made unto us...redemption" (1 Cor. 1:30). Flavel believes that the term "redemption" refers to glorification: the "hope of the glory of God" (Rom. 5:2). Elsewhere, Paul writes, "For our conversation is in heaven; from whence also we look for the Saviour, the Lord Jesus Christ: who shall change our vile body, that it may be fashioned like unto his glorious body, according to the working whereby he is able even to subdue all things unto himself" (Phil. 3:20-21; also see Col. 3:4). According to Flavel, this transformation (glorification) will mark our release from seven chains. (1) We will be free from "defiling corruptions."[26] The guilt of sin is pardoned by justification and the power of sin is broken by sanctification, but the presence of sin is removed only at glorification. At that

---

24. Flavel, *Works*, II:17.

25. Hall, *Christ Mystical*, 113.

26. Flavel, *Works*, III:113.

time, the lusts of the flesh and mind will be gone. We will enter a state of "perfect purity." (2) We will be free from "sinking sorrows."[27] At present, because of affliction, we cry with Naomi: "Call me not Naomi [*pleasant*], call me Mara [*bitter*]" (Ruth 1:20). But the day is coming when we will be free from all suffering. As John records, "And God shall wipe away all tears from their eyes; and there shall be no more death, neither sorrow, nor crying, neither shall there be any more pain: for the former things are passed away" (Rev. 21:4). We will enter a state of "fullness of joy." (3) We will be free from "entangling temptations."[28] The devil is relentless in his assault "against our souls." However, in the future, "he can no more touch or affect the soul with any temptation, than we can better the body of the sun with snow-balls." We will enter a state of "everlasting freedom." (4) We will be free from "distressing persecutions."[29] "We must spend our days," says Flavel, "under the oppression of the wicked; yet this is our comfort, we know when we shall be far enough out of their reach." At that time, we will enter a state of "full and perfect rest." (5) We will be free from "pinching wants."[30] We have temporal wants. More importantly, we have spiritual wants. We lack faith, joy, peace, love, and zeal. Plus, we struggle in spiritual duties. These deficiencies plague us. At glorification, however, every want will be supplied. We will enter a state of "universal supplies." (6) We will be free from "distracting fears."[31] Flavel classifies these fears according to "body" and "soul." In that day, "no wind of fear shall ever ruffle or disturb their souls, and put them into a storm any more." We will enter a state of "highest security and rest." (7) We will be free from "deluding shadows."[32] These are the deceitful vani-

---

27. Flavel, *Works*, III:114.
28. Flavel, *Works*, III:114.
29. Flavel, *Works*, III:115.
30. Flavel, *Works*, III:115.
31. Flavel, *Works*, III:116.
32. Flavel, *Works*, III:117.

ties of the world. "Vanity of vanities, saith the preacher; all is vanity" (Eccl. 12:8). These deluding shadows tempt believers at present. One day, however, they will be but a shadow of a memory. And we will enter a state of "substantial good."

Conclusion

When Christ takes hold of us by His Spirit and we take hold of Him by our faith, we become one. By virtue of this mystical union, we partake of the blessings procured through the hypostatic union. As Flavel makes clear, "It is Christ himself who is made all this unto us: we can have no saving benefit separate and apart from the person of Christ: many would willingly receive his *privileges*, who will not receive his person; but it cannot be; if we will have one, we must take the other too: Yea, we must accept his person first, and then his benefits: as it is in the marriage covenant, so it is here."[33]

Because of our union with Christ's person, we partake of the blessings of His prophetic office: He has become to us wisdom. Because of our union with Christ's person, we partake of the blessings of His priestly office: He has become to us righteousness. Because of our union with Christ's person, we partake of the blessings of His kingly office: He has become to us sanctification and redemption. For Flavel, these four blessings correspond to "a fourfold misery lying upon sinful man, *viz.* ignorance, guilt, pollution, and the whole train of miserable consequences and effects, let in upon the nature of men."[34] Because these four blessings remove this "fourfold misery," they "take in all that is necessary or desirable, to make a soul truly and perfectly blessed."[35]

33. Flavel, *Works*, II:17.

34. Flavel, *Works*, II:16.

35. Flavel, *Works*, II:17. Hall agrees, "As thus Christ is made unto us Wisdom, Righteousness, Sanctification, and Redemption, so whatsoever else he either is, or hath, or doth, by virtue of this blessed union becomes ours.... He is all to us, and all is ours in him" (*Christ Mystical*, 116-17).

Chapter 6

THE FRUIT OF UNION
WITH CHRIST

Because of our union with Christ's person, we have "communion with Christ in his righteousness, by the way of imputation; we partake of his holiness, by the way of infusion; and of his glory in heaven, by the beatifical vision."[1] Again, Flavel says, "By imputed righteousness, we are freed from the guilt of sin: by imparted holiness, we are freed from the dominion of sin, and by our glorification with Christ, we are freed from all the relics and remains both of sin and misery let in by sin upon our natures."[2] This paradigm is significant, because it means that Flavel views justification as a "relative" change, sanctification as a "real" change, and glorification as a "perfect" change.

The above implies that when it comes to discerning the Holy Spirit's work upon our souls, sanctification is of first importance: it is a "real" change that produces visible fruit. In this chapter, we turn our attention to what Flavel has to say about this subject. I will expound his insights in the context of Romans 7:1-6.[3]

Marriage to Christ
Paul begins in verse 1, asking, "Know ye not, brethren…how that the law hath dominion over a man as long as he liveth?" Here, Paul establishes two principles that are foundational

---

1. Flavel, *Works*, II:149.

2. Flavel, *Works*, II:149; also see II:25.

3. For Pearse's thoughts on these verses, see *Best Match*, 34-38.

to his main argument in these verses: (1) law has jurisdiction over us; and (2) death frees us from law's jurisdiction.

In verses 2-3,[4] Paul uses marriage to illustrate these two principles. (1) The principle that law has jurisdiction over us is seen in the fact that a woman is under the jurisdiction (dominion or authority) of her husband. According to the law, she is bound to him as long as he lives. As a matter of fact, if "she be married to another man, she shall be called an adulteress." (2) The principle that death frees us from law's jurisdiction is seen in the fact that a woman is released from her husband's jurisdiction if he dies. If that happens, she is free to enter into a new relationship.

In verse 4,[5] Paul arrives at his main point, saying that the Law (as a covenant of works) has jurisdiction over us. However, just as death ends the jurisdiction of a husband over his wife, even so death ends the Law's jurisdiction over us. Paul's point is this: Christ died, thereby satisfying the Law's penalty; and God reckons us dead to the Law, because we are one with Christ. Having been released from the Law's jurisdiction through Christ's death, we are free to "be married to another, *even* to him who is raised from the dead." Commenting on these verses, Flavel states:

> One end of Christ's death was, to purchase our free-
> dom, that we might be capable of being espoused to
> him; for you must know that we were not in a capac-
> ity whilst under the curse of the law, to be married

---

4. "For the woman which hath an husband is bound by the law to her husband as long as he liveth; but if the husband be dead, she is loosed from the law of her husband. So then if, while her husband liveth, she be married to another man, she shall be called an adulteress: but if her husband be dead, she is free from that law; so that she is no adulteress, though she be married to another man."

5. "Wherefore, my brethren, ye also are become dead to the law by the body of Christ, that ye should be married to another, even to him who is raised from the dead, that we should bring forth fruit unto God."

unto Christ: the apostle (Rom. 7:2-4) compares the law to a husband, to whom the wife is bound as long as he liveth, and not capable of a second marriage until her husband be dead. The death of Christ was the death of the law, as a covenant of works holding us under the bond of the curse of it.[6]

Fruit for Death

According to verse 5,[7] prior to our marriage to Christ, we produced only "fruit unto death." The reason for this is the fact that, in a state of "degeneration," the will is controlled by an understanding that prefers darkness to light and by affections that prefer evil to good. In this state, the soul is incapable of doing anything "morally" good, because it lacks love for God. This view of the effect of Adam's fall upon humanity is known as the Augustinian principle, which Calvin states as follows: "The natural gifts in men were corrupted, but the supernatural taken away."[8] The "natural gifts" are the faculties of the soul (or the natural image of God) whereas the "supernatural gifts" are knowledge, righteousness, and holiness (or the moral image of God).[9] By virtue of Adam's

---

6. Flavel, *Works*, IV:122.

7. "For when we were in the flesh, the motions of sins, which were by the law, did work in our members to bring forth fruit unto death."

8. Calvin, *Institutes*, II.II.4, 12, 14, 18.

9. See Eph. 4:24 and Col. 3:10. There is some controversy surrounding the place of the Augustinian principle in Calvin's thought. Dewey Hoitenga maintains that Calvin's adherence to the Augustinian principle necessarily implies that when he "comes to describe the components of the will and intellect in their fallen state, he will need to include the very components he attributes to them in their created state—even though neither power is any longer sound and whole, but weakened and corrupted" (*John Calvin and the Will: A Critique and Corrective* [Grand Rapids: Baker Books, 1997], 73). In short, this means that the mind must retain its ability to discern between good and evil whereas the will must retain its ability to choose between good and evil because it possesses "something of its created inclination to goodness besides its new inclination to evil." However, Hoitenga

fall, we have lost the moral image of God. The natural image, however, remains. We still possess understanding, affections, and will, but these faculties never function from a right principle, because the moral image of God is lost. For this reason, our choices are never good in God's sight.[10]

Flavel adopts the Augustinian principle, being careful to distinguish between "civil" and "moral" goodness. Simply put, a deed may be "civilly" good (i.e., good in man's sight) without being "morally" good (i.e., good in God's sight). Whether a deed is "morally" good or evil is determined by the principle from which it flows. Unbelievers do not love God; therefore, their deeds are never good in God's sight. Flavel comments, "Unregenerate men, who never were acquainted with the mystery of spiritual union with Jesus Christ, but still grow upon their natural root, old Adam, may, by the force and power of natural principles, bring forth some fruit, which, like the wild hedge-fruit we speak of, may, indeed, be fair and pleasant to the eyes of men, but God takes no pleasure at all in it; it is sour, harsh, and distasteful to him, because it springs not from the Spirit of Christ."[11] Again, "This corrupt root spoils the fruit, by the transmission of its sour and naughty sap into all the branches and fruits that grow upon it...no mere natural or unregenerate man can ever do one holy or acceptable action, because the corruption of the root is in all those actions."[12]

---

argues that Calvin fails to do precisely this, thereby revealing a glaring inconsistency in his thought (*John Calvin and the Will*, 84). For the opposite view, see I. John Hesselink, *Calvin's Concept of the Law* (Allison Park: Pickwick Publications, 1992), 64-65; and Anthony Lane, "Did Calvin Believe in Free Will?" *Vox Evangelica* 12 (1981): 72-90; and Thomas Torrance, *Calvin's Doctrine of Man* (Grand Rapids: Eerdmans, 1957), 88-94.

10. Calvin, *Institutes*, I.V.6; II.I.11; II.II.13; II.II.3; III.XIV.2.

11. Flavel, *Works*, V:141-42.

12. Flavel, *Works*, V:142.

While married to the Law under the covenant of works, we were—as Paul makes clear in verse 5—"in the flesh." Therefore, we lacked the necessary principle (i.e., love for God) to produce fruit for God. To put it simply, our fruit was unacceptable to Him. As Stephen Charnock[13] makes clear, "All fruit before marriage is bastard."[14] In a similar vein, Flavel remarks, "But that which is highly esteemed of men, is abomination to God (Luke 16:15). It finds no acceptance with him, because it springs from that cursed root of nature, and is not the production of his own Spirit."[15]

Fruit for God

Now that we are married to Christ, we produce fruit by the Holy Spirit. In verse 6, Paul says, "We serve in newness of spirit and not in the oldness of the letter" (Rom. 7:6). The "oldness of the letter" is life with the old husband under the covenant of works whereas the "newness of spirit" is life with the new husband under the covenant of grace. This new marriage produces what Paul calls, in verse 4, "fruit unto God."

For Flavel, the essence of this fruit is Christ-likeness, which he views as consisting of eight "patterns."[16] (1) Christ's "purity and holiness."[17] There is a two-fold holiness in Christ: His nature and practice. Similarly, we should be holy in the "principle" of our heart and the "practice" of our life.

---

13. Stephen Charnock (1628-1680) was a graduate of Cambridge (B.A.) and Oxford (M.A.), and held several pastorates. He is best known for his treatise, *Discourses Upon the Existence and Attributes of God*.

14. Stephen Charnock, *Discourses Upon the Existence and Attributes of God: Vol. I-II* (London: Robert Carter & Brothers, 1853; rpt., Grand Rapids: Baker Books, 1990), I:505.

15. Flavel, *Works*, V:143.

16. These are found in Flavel's sermon, "Of the Imitation of Christ in holiness of Life, and the necessity of it in Believers," in his treatise, *The Method of Grace*, *Works*, II:397-413. It is based upon 1 John 2:6, where John states, "He that saith he abideth in him, ought himself also so to walk, even as he walked."

17. Flavel, *Works*, II:402. See 1 Peter 1:15-16.

(2) Christ's "obedience to his Father's will."[18] It was "free and voluntary," "universal and complete," and "sincere and pure." It flowed from "the spring and fountain of ardent love to God." We too should obey God as an expression of our love for Him. (3) Christ's "self-denial."[19] "What did he not deny," asks Flavel, "when he left the bosom of his Father, with the ineffable delights and pleasures he there enjoyed from eternity, and instead thereof to drink the cup, the bitter cup of his Father's wrath, for our sakes?" We should follow Christ's example by denying our "natural self" (our life in competition with God's glory), our "civil self" (our relations in the world), and our "moral self" (our self-righteousness). (4) Christ's "activity and diligence in finishing the work of God."[20] His heart was set upon it. This is seen in the fact that He never fainted despite many discouragements, and He improved all opportunities to further His work. In a similar vein, we should not "trifle away" our lives in "vanity." (5) Christ's "delight in God, and in his service."[21] Christ says, "My meat is to do the will of him that sent me, and to finish his work" (John 4:34). We too should delight in God and His service. (6) Christ's "inoffensiveness" in His life upon earth.[22] He was "holy and harmless." He injured and offended none. Likewise, we should strive to be inoffensive in our conduct. (7) Christ's "humility and lowliness."[23] This is seen in His "stooping down from all his glory to a state of the deepest contempt, for the glory of God and our salvation." According to Flavel, we should show humility in our habits, company, and language. (8) Christ's contentment in assuming "a low and mean condition in the world."[24] Flavel

18. Flavel, *Works*, II:404. See Heb. 5:8.

19. Flavel, *Works*, II:406. See 2 Cor. 8:9.

20. Flavel, *Works*, II:407. See Acts 10:38.

21. Flavel, *Works*, II:409. See John 4:34.

22. Flavel, *Works*, II:410. See Heb. 7:26.

23. Flavel, *Works*, II:411. See Matt. 11:29.

24. Flavel, *Works*, II:412. See Isa. 53:7.

remarks, "His lot in this world fell upon a condition of deepest poverty and contempt." Like Christ, we should seek "to manage an afflicted condition with a contented spirit."

Conclusion

By His Spirit, Christ produces the above fruit in us. For Flavel, it cannot be otherwise, for as Christ says to His disciples: "I am the vine, ye are the branches: He that abideth in me, and I in him, the same bringeth forth much fruit: for without me ye can do nothing" (John 15:5). Just as the character of the vine is produced in the fruit of the branches, even so Christ's character is produced in us. This is the "real" change of sanctification. Handley Moule[25] provides an insightful summary to this entire discussion when he writes:

> Joined to the Second Man, the last Adam of Resurrection, the people of God, by a blessed naturalness of result, are to be productive of thought, word, and act in his interest, for his praise, and because of their union with his life. By a sequence as natural (in a true sense) as that by which sinning resulted from their inheritance of the life of self, well-doing unto the Lord is to result from their union to the life of their Redeemer. There is that in their holy Union with him which is divinely calculated thus to come out in a life of true holiness; and they are to act upon that fact, in the restful strength of those who know that they do possess a wholly supernatural endowment for these new results.[26]

25. Handley Moule (1841-1920) was Bishop of Durham. He was also a leading influence for Evangelicalism at Cambridge.

26. Handley Moule, *Thoughts on Union with Christ* (London: Seeley & Co. Limited, 1885), 58.

Chapter 7

———— ⸻《◉》⸻ ————

THE EVIDENCE OF UNION WITH CHRIST

Flavel is firm in his conviction that union with Christ results in "fruit unto God." "There are," he affirms, "no barren branches growing upon this fruitful root."[1] The implication of this is obvious: if we are not Christ-like, then we have no reason to think that we are one with Him. Paul says that Christ "loved the church, and gave himself for it; that he might sanctify and cleanse it with the washing of water by the word, that he might present it to himself a glorious church, not having spot, or wrinkle, or any such thing; but that it should be holy and without blemish" (Eph. 5:25-27). There are three important details in these verses. (1) Christ unites Himself to His bride so that He might "sanctify" and "cleanse" her. The act of sanctifying is positive; He sets His bride apart for Himself. The act of cleansing is negative; He cleanses His bride from her sin. (2) Christ accomplishes this cleansing with "the washing of water by the word." Hence, God's Word is the means by which her cleansing is effected.[2] (3) Christ's goal in sanctifying and cleansing His bride is to present her to Himself, "not having spot, or wrinkle or any such thing; but that it should be holy and without blemish."

For Flavel, Christ's purpose for His bride necessarily implies that the believer's mystical union with Christ will be evident for all to see. If there is no visible fruit, it is because there is no union. He warns that there is a "difference

1. Flavel, *Works*, II:48.
2. See John 15:3; 17:7; James 1:18; 1 Peter 1:23.

between those who, by profession and common estimation, pass for Christians among men, though they have no other union with Christ, but by an *external adhesion* to him in the external duties of religion, and those whose union with Christ is real, vital, and permanent, by the indwelling of the Spirit of Christ in their souls."[3] With this difference before him, he exhorts his readers to examine themselves in order to make certain that they are in Christ:

> Examine your relations to Christ. Are you his *spouse*? Have you forsaken all for him? Are you ready to take your lot with him, as it falls in prosperity or adversity? Are you loyal to Christ? Do you yield obedience to him as your Head and Husband? Are you his spiritual seed, his children by regeneration? Are you born of the Spirit? Do you resemble Christ in holiness? Do you find a reverential fear of Christ carrying you to obey him in all things? Are you led by the Spirit of Christ? To conclude, Have you the *spirit of adoption*, enabling you to cry, *Abba, Father*?[4]

My purpose in this chapter is to consider Flavel's call to self-examination. In *The Method of Grace*, he devotes a sermon to the subject, based upon 1 John 3:24, where John states, "And he that keepeth his commandments dwelleth in him, and he in him. And hereby we know that he abideth in us, by the Spirit which he hath given us."[5] Flavel divides

---

3. Flavel, *Works*, II:328. In *A Treatise of the Soul of Man*, Flavel expounds twelve "ways to hell." The seventh is "groundless presumption." The eleventh is "formal hypocrisy in religion." The twelfth is "mere civility and moral honesty" (*Works*, III:201, 214, 216).

4. Flavel, *Works*, I:482.

5. The sermon is entitled, "An Interest in Christ known by the Gift of the Holy Spirit, and His operations in the Soul," in *Works*, II:328-44. This is one of seven sermons in *The Method of Grace*, in which Flavel seeks to distinguish between true and nominal Christians (*Works*, II:328-421). For more on this subject, see Flavel's treatise, *The Touchstone of Sincerity; or, The Signs of Grace and the Symptoms of Hypocrisy*, in *Works*, V:509-603.

this verse into three parts. (1) There is the thing to be tried: "he abideth in us." We must determine "whether we stand in Christ as dead branches in a living stock, which are only bound to it by external ligatures or bonds that hold them for a while together; or whether our souls have a vital union and coalition with Christ, by the participation of the living sap of that blessed root."[6] (2) There is the trial of this union: "by the Spirit which he hath given us." All those who are one with Christ possess the Holy Spirit. (3) There is the certainty of this trial: "hereby we know." Although the soul's union with Christ is a "supernatural mystery," "it is discoverable by the effects thereof."[7] Flavel proceeds to identify seven such "effects."

A Convicting Spirit

First, "in whomsoever the Spirit of Christ is a Spirit of sanctification, to that man or woman he hath been, more or less, a Spirit of conviction and humiliation."[8] Again, "Where there are no blossoms, we can expect no fruit; and where we see no conviction of sin, we can expect no conversion to Christ. Hath then the Spirit of God been a Spirit of conviction to thee?"[9] Flavel's reasoning is simple: the Holy Spirit is a convicting Spirit; therefore, those who are under true conviction of sin possess the Holy Spirit.[10] This conclusion stems from Flavel's belief that the Holy Spirit works in the soul by certain steps (or degrees) prior to conversion.[11] The

---

6. Flavel, *Works*, II:329.

7. Flavel, *Works*, II:330.

8. Flavel, *Works*, II:336.

9. Flavel, *Works*, II:336; also see II:61-62,101; IV:192.

10. Flavel equates this pre-conversion work of the Holy Spirit with the preaching of the Law. He devotes four sermons to this subject in *The Method of Grace*, *Works*, II:287-327.

11. Flavel's comments should not be confused with preparationism. He writes, "I pity many poor souls upon this account, who stand off from Christ, dare not believe because they want such and such quali-

principal steps are illumination, conviction, and compunction.[12] These steps are necessary, because (as noted earlier) our free will is in bondage to sin. Christ declares, "Come unto me, all ye that labour and are heavy-laden, and I will give you rest" (Matt. 11:28). However, we will not respond to Christ's call until we feel "heavy-laden." And we will never feel "heavy-laden" until the Holy Spirit produces illumination, conviction, and compunction. Once this happens, we are ready to cry, "What shall we do?" (Acts 2:37). "In this order," writes Flavel, "the Spirit (ordinarily) draws souls to Christ, he shines into their minds by illumination; applies that light to their consciences by effectual conviction; breaks and wounds their hearts for sin by compunction; and then moves the will to embrace and close with Christ in the way of faith for life and salvation."[13] For Flavel, therefore, we may know if we are in Christ by simply looking for these "antecedents" to conversion.

A Quickening Spirit

Second, "the Spirit of God…is a quickening Spirit, to all those to whom he is given." Having been born again, our affections are rightly ordered, meaning our love is set upon God. When separated from God, therefore, the soul experiences "desire and hope to…quicken its motion towards him."[14] When the soul encounters anything that impedes its fellowship with God, it experiences "fear, grief, indignation, jealousy, anger, &c."[15] When in communion with God, the

---

fications to fit them for Christ. O saith one, could I find so much brokenness of heart for sin, so much reformation and power over corruptions, then I could come to Christ; the meaning of which is this, if I could bring a price in my hand to purchase him, then I should be encouraged to go unto him. Here now lies horrible pride covered over with a veil of great humility" (*Works*, IV:57; also see I:187).

12. Flavel, *Works*, II:336; also see II:129-30.

13. Flavel, *Works*, II:71.

14. Flavel, *Works*, II:509.

15. Flavel, *Works*, II:510.

soul experiences "love, delight, and joy, whereby it rests in him."[16] As a result of these well-directed affections, the soul is drawn away from sin to God. For Flavel, this inclination is evident in "spiritual motions"[17] such as feeling the burden of sin, hungering and thirsting after righteousness, and engaging in spiritual conflicts with sin. These spiritual "senses" point to spiritual life in the soul, which points to the indwelling of the Holy Spirit, which points to union with Christ.[18] Flavel exhorts, "Spiritual life hath its spiritual senses, and suitable operations. O think upon this you that cannot feel any burden in sin, you that have no hungerings or thirstings after Christ; how can the Spirit of God be in you?"[19]

A Loving Spirit

Third, "those to whom God giveth his Spirit have a tender sympathy with all the interests and concernments of Christ."[20] In simple terms, Flavel means that if we are partakers of the Holy Spirit, then we love what He loves and hate what He hates.[21] For starters, we love Christ: "They that are so nearly united to him, as members to the head, cannot but love him and value him above their own lives."[22] This love is not motivated by what we receive from Him, but by who He is. True love is focused upon an object's goodness, not any perceived personal benefits derived from it. As Charnock warns, "To love God only for his benefits, is to love ourselves first, and him secondarily: to love God for his

---

16. Flavel, *Works*, II:510.

17. Flavel, *Works*, IV:192.

18. Flavel, *Works*, II:101. Pearse declares, "Surely, there is more sweetness, more happiness, in one kiss of the mouth of this blessed Lord, in one embrace in his bosom, one moment's communion with him, than in all the delights of sin and the creature" (*Best Match*, 52).

19. Flavel, *Works*, II:337; also see II:101.

20. Flavel, *Works*, II:337; also see II:134.

21. Flavel, *Works*, II:337.

22. Flavel, *Works*, II:48.

own goodness and excellency, is a true love of God; a love of him for himself."[23]

Flowing from our love for God is love for God's people. "Religion," says Flavel, "breeds bowels of compassion."[24] He declares, "What, at peace with the Father, and at war with the children? It cannot be.... Surely, in that day we are reconciled to the Lord, we are reconciled to all his people: we all then love a Christian as a Christian, and by this we may know that we are passed from life unto death."[25] With this love before him, Flavel asks his readers to examine themselves: "Is it thus with thee? Dost thou sympathize with the affairs and concernments of Christ in the world? Or, carest thou not which way things go with the people of God, and gospel of Christ, so long as thine own affairs prosper, and all things are well with thee?"[26]

A Mortifying Spirit

Fourth, "wherever the Spirit of God dwelleth, he doth in some degree, mortify and subdue the evils and corruptions of the soul in which he resides."[27] Flavel makes it clear that mortification is not "the total abolition of sin," "the suppression of the external acts of sin," "the cessation of the external acts of sin," or "the severe castigation of the body."[28] Rather, it is the "subversion" of sin's dominion in the soul.[29] By virtue of our union with Christ, the understanding is illuminated, the affections are softened, and the will is liberated. Therefore, sin's dominion is broken. As Flavel makes clear, "The Spirit of God implants habits of a contrary nature,

---

23. Charnock, *Existence and Attributes of God*, II:333; also see I:148-50.

24. Flavel, *Works*, IV:234.

25. Flavel, *Works*, II:63.

26. Flavel, *Works*, II:338.

27. Flavel, *Works*, II:338; also see II:134, 365.

28. Flavel, *Works*, II:370-71.

29. Flavel, *Works*, II:372.

which are destructive to sin, and are purgative of corruption."[30] This means that "grace gives the mind and heart of a man a contrary bent and inclination," and "holy principles destroy the interest that sin once had in the love and delight of the soul."

This is the experience of all those who are in Christ. As Flavel says, "We cannot be united with this root, and not partake of the vital sap of sanctification from him."[31] Paul makes that clear in Romans 8:13, where he states, "If ye through the Spirit do mortify the deeds of the body, ye shall live." For Flavel, the implication of Paul's words is this: "The design of every true believer, is co-incident with the design of the Spirit, to destroy and mortify corruption: They long after the extirpation of it, and are daily in the use of all sanctified means and instruments, to subdue and destroy it."[32] If there is no desire to mortify sin, then there is no union with Christ. The sad reality is that many professing believers lack this desire. "Many are afraid of burning," says Flavel, "that never were afraid of sinning."[33] They are driven to profess faith in Christ by a fear of hell, not a fear of sin. For Flavel, that is a sure sign of an unregenerate heart. He declares, "There be many that do but trifle in religion, and play about the skirts and borders of it...but as to the power of religion, and the life of godliness, which consist in communion with God in duties and ordinances, which promote holiness, and mortify their lusts, they concern not themselves about these things."[34]

On this basis, Flavel exhorts us to examine ourselves. Do we possess a mortifying spirit? "It is manifest in many of us, that we are no enemies to sin; we secretly indulge it, what bad names soever we call it. We will commit ten sins to cover

---

30. Flavel, *Works*, II:378.
31. Flavel, *Works*, II:48.
32. Flavel, *Works*, II:338; also see II:101-02.
33. Flavel, *Works*, II:179.
34. Flavel, *Works*, I:209.

one: we cannot endure the most serious, faithful, seasonable, private, tender, and necessary reproofs for sin, but our hearts swell and rise at it; sure we are not reconciled to God, whilst we embrace his enemy in our bosoms."[35]

A Praying Spirit

Fifth, "wherever the Spirit of God dwelleth in the way of sanctification, in all such he is the Spirit of prayer and supplication."[36] The Holy Spirit inclines the soul to pray—to commune with the object of its love: God. He also assists the soul in prayer by "setting an edge" upon our "desires and affections."[37] If, therefore, we have a desire to pray, we can be sure that the Holy Spirit dwells within us. "A spirit of prayer," remarks Flavel, "is an evidence of spiritual life, as the effect of Christ's voice to the soul."[38] George Swinnock[39] shares the same conviction, asking his readers:

> Doth the Spirit of God bring thee often upon thy knees? Art thou one of the generation of seekers? Art thou one of God's suppliants? Dost thou know what it is to be poor in spirit, to be a beggar, and to live altogether upon the alms-basket of heaven's bounty? Is there a constant trade driven betwixt God and thy soul—God sending down mercies, and thou sending up prayers? This is the daily exchange. Canst thou better live without thy daily bread than this daily duty? When thy heart is big with grief, whither dost thou go? Is this thy great ease, that thou mayest empty thy soul into God's ears?[40]

---

35. Flavel, *Works*, II:63.

36. Flavel, *Works*, II:338.

37. Flavel, *Works*, II:338.

38. Flavel, *Works*, II:192.

39. George Swinnock (1627-1673) graduated from Cambridge (B.A.) and Oxford (M.A.). He ministered at several churches until his ejection from the Church of England for Nonconformity in 1662.

40. George Swinnock, *The Works of George Swinnock: Vol. I-V*, ed. James Nichol (London, 1868; rpt., Edinburgh: Banner of Truth,

Flavel drives home the same point when he writes, "The new creature is a praying creature, living by its daily communion with God, which is its livelihood and subsistence (Zech. 12:10; Acts 9:11). If, therefore, thou be a prayerless soul, or if, in all thy prayers, thou art a stranger to communion with God; if there be no brokenness of heart for sin in thy confessions, no melting affections for Christ and holiness in thy supplications; surely Satan doth but baffle and delude thy over-credulous soul, in persuading thee that thou art a new creature."[41]

A Heavenly Minded Spirit

Sixth, "wherever the Spirit of grace inhabits, there is an heavenly, spiritual frame of mind accompanying, and evidencing the indwelling of the Spirit."[42] Again, "If thou hast seen the beauty, felt the power, and heard the voice of Christ, thy soul like an uncentered body, will be still propending, gravitating, and inclining Christward.... A sweeter sign of thy hearing Christ's voice can hardly be found in a soul of man, than restless longing to be with Christ in the state of perfect freedom from sin, and full fruition of the beloved and blessed Jesus."[43] Underlying this conviction is Flavel's belief that "the workings of every creature follow the being and nature of it."[44] This means that if we are carnal, we are inclined to what is earthly. If, however, we are spiritual, we are inclined to what is heavenly.

On that basis, we can determine whether or not we are united with Christ. Where the Holy Spirit dwells, there is necessarily a heavenly frame of mind. "The mind and affections of the new creature," explains Flavel, "are set upon

1992), III:303.
41. Flavel, *Works*, II:366.
42. Flavel, *Works*, II:339.
43. Flavel, *Works*, IV:193.
44. Flavel, *Works*, II:339.

heavenly and spiritual things (Col. 3:1-2; Eph. 4:23; Rom. 8:5). If, therefore, thy heart and affections be habitually earthly and wholly intent upon things below, driving eagerly after the world, as the great business and end of thy life, deceive not thyself, this is not the fruit of the new creature, nor consistent with it."[45]

An Obeying Spirit

Seventh, "those to whom the Spirit of grace is given, are led by the Spirit."[46] Flavel adds, "Sanctified souls give themselves up to the government and conduct of the Spirit; they obey his voice, beg his direction, follow his motions, deny the solicitations of flesh and blood, in obedience to him."[47] "In vain," therefore, "do we claim union with Christ as our head, whilst we are governed by our own wills, and our lusts give us law."[48]

Flavel is careful to point out that such obedience should not be confused with legalism: it is "no bondage; for the law is not only written in Christ's statute-book, the Bible, but copied out by his Spirit upon the hearts of his subjects, in correspondent principles; which makes obedience a pleasure, and self-denial easy."[49] For Flavel, therefore, there is no antithesis between law and gospel. Having been justified

---

45. Flavel, *Works*, II:366.

46. Flavel, *Works*, II:340; also see II:134.

47. Flavel, *Works*, II:340.

48. Flavel, *Works*, II:48.

49. Flavel, *Works*, I:203. This emphasis among the Puritans often results in the erroneous charge of "legalism." However, as Ernest Kevan rightly acknowledges, "Legalism is the abuse of the Law as a means of obtaining a meritorious standing before God; it is the use of the Law 'as pharisaically conceived,' and an employment of it in its outward form without regard to its inward demands.... The 'legalism' of Puritanism is a 'bogey' constructed by prejudiced imagination from the popular caricature of the God-fearing Puritan and from ignorance of what he taught" (*The Grace of Law* [Ligonier: Soli Deo Gloria, 1993], 259).

by faith, we are bound to obey the law in accordance with the New Covenant. He states, "Christ doth not free believers from obedience to the moral law: It is true we are no more under it as a covenant for our justification; but we are, and must still be under it, as a rule for our direction."[50] This is in line with the *WCF*, which states that obedience is not "contrary to the grace of the gospel," because it is "the Spirit of Christ subduing and enabling the will of man to do that freely and cheerfully which the will of God, revealed in the law, requireth to be done."[51]

In short, the person who delights in God also delights in obeying God. In this regard, Ernest Kevan rightly concludes that, for the Puritans, "Only the heart that can say, 'I delight to do thy will, O my God' (Ps. 40:8), can be adjudged to be truly converted and godly."[52] This is certainly Flavel's conviction. As Paul says, "For as many as are led by the Spirit of God, they are the sons of God" (Rom. 8:14). If, therefore, we desire to obey God and delight in doing so, we can be certain that the Holy Spirit dwells within.

Conclusion

For Flavel, the above seven "effects" are the essence of assurance.[53] Paul says, "The Spirit itself beareth witness with our spirit, that we are the children of God" (Rom. 8:16). In commenting on the Puritan understanding of this verse, Packer writes, "The Puritans identified 'our spirit' with the Christian's conscience, which, with the Spirit's aid, is able to discern in his heart the marks which Scripture specifies as tokens of the new birth and to conclude from them that he is

---

50. Flavel, *Works*, II:271; also see I:439, III:551.

51. *WCF*, XIX:VII.

52. Kevan, *Grace of Law*, 183.

53. For a full treatment of the Puritan doctrine of assurance, see Joel R. Beeke, *Assurance of Faith: Calvin, English Puritanism, and the Dutch Second Reformation* (New York: Peter Lang, 1991).

a child of God."[54] In this paradigm, the Holy Spirit both provides the evidence (i.e., the marks of grace) and empowers the individual's reason to evaluate it. Flavel agrees, affirming that the Holy Spirit testifies to our salvation in two ways: (1) "objectively, i.e. by working those graces in our souls which are the conditions of the promise, and so the Spirit and his graces in us, are all one"; and (2) "effectively, i.e. by irradiating the soul with a grace-discovering light, shining upon his own work."[55]

The above seven "effects" (or graces) are, for Flavel, evidence that the Spirit of sanctification resides within. This indwelling presence of the Spirit is, in turn, evidence that we are one with Christ. As John says, "And hereby we know that he abideth in us, by the Spirit which he hath given us" (1 John 3:24). The implication for Flavel is clear: "None can claim benefit by imputed righteousness, but those only that live in the power of inherent holiness: to whomsoever Christ is made righteousness, to him he also is made sanctification."[56]

---

54. Packer, *Quest for Godliness*, 183.

55. Flavel, *Works*, V:434.

56. Flavel, *Works*, II:27.

Chapter 8

━━━━ •((•))• ━━━

THE SUFFERING OF UNION
WITH CHRIST

In addition to the seven "effects" considered in the previous chapter, Flavel asserts that the believer's mystical union with Christ is made evident by persevering in the midst of affliction. By "affliction," he has in view the suffering that arises from union with Christ. As Paul writes, "[I] rejoice in my sufferings for you, and fill up that which is behind of the afflictions of Christ in my flesh for his body's sake, which is the church" (Col. 1:24). Regarding this verse, Flavel remarks:

> He suffered once in *corpore proprio*, in his own person, as Mediator; these sufferings are complete and full, and in that sense he suffers no more: he suffers also in *corpore mystico*, in his church and members, thus he still suffers in the sufferings of every saint for his sake; and though these sufferings in his mystical body are not equal to the other, either *pondere et mensura*, in their weight and value, nor yet designed *ex officio*, for the same use and purpose, to satisfy by their proper merit, offended justice; nevertheless they are truly reckoned the sufferings of Christ, because the head suffers when the members do.[1]

Here, Flavel makes it clear that Paul is not suggesting that something is lacking in Christ's atoning work. The term "affliction" (θλιψις) is never used in reference to Christ's suffering on the cross; rather, it is used to describe the tribulations that He encountered during the course of His life.

---

1. Flavel, *Works*, II:36-37; also see II:151, VI:9.

He experienced opposition, persecution, and rejection in this world. He continues to do so through His mystical body —the church.

As far as Paul is concerned, it is a joy to fill up what is "behind" (or lacking) in Christ's afflictions. Elsewhere, he says, "we glory in our tribulations" (Rom. 5:3). Similarly, James writes, "My brethren, count it all joy when ye fall into divers temptations" (James 1:2). And Peter declares, "Wherein ye greatly rejoice, though now for a season, if need be, ye are in heaviness through manifold temptations" (1 Peter 1:6). How is it possible to rejoice in suffering? Gathering together Flavel's thoughts on the subject, we discover that we must embrace three truths.

God's Promise
First, we must embrace God's promise. Here, Flavel is primarily thinking of Romans 8:28, where Paul writes, "And we know that all things work together for good to them that love God, to them who are the called according to his purpose."[2] Flavel is careful to point out that here the term "good" refers to God's plan to glorify His name by conforming us to the likeness of Christ.[3] This observation is important, because it sets parameters for the promise. "The intent of the Redeemer's undertaking," Flavel writes, "was not to purchase for his people riches, ease, and pleasures on earth; but to mortify their lusts, heal their natures, and spiritualize their affections; and thereby fit them for the eternal fruition of God."[4] God promises to work all things together for this good.

---

2. (1) "We know." This implies "certainty." (2) "That all things." These include ordinances, promises, blessings, afflictions, temptations, corruptions, and desertions. (3) "Work together." They are "over-ruled and determined to such an issue by the gracious hand of God" (Flavel, *Works*, V:279-80).

3. See Rom. 8:29.

4. Flavel, *Works*, VI:84.

For Flavel, this promise must be kept in view when suffering arises, for it is "the compass which sets the course, and directs the motions of all the afflictions of the people of God; and no ship at sea obeys the rudder so exactly, as the troubles of the righteous do the direction of this promise. Possibly we cannot discern this at present, but rather prejudge the works of God, and say all these things are against us; but hereafter we shall see, and with joy acknowledge them to be the happy instruments of our salvation."[5]

Flavel's conviction that God "directs the motions" of His people's afflictions for their good arises from his view of God's providence. On the one hand, there is God's "general" governance, "exercised about all creatures, rational and irrational, animate and inanimate." On the other hand, there is God's "special and peculiar" governance, exercised over the church by way of "union and special influence." What is the relationship between the two? According to Flavel, "The church is his *special* care and charge; he rules the world for her good, as an head consulting the welfare of the body."[6] In other words, God governs His "general" kingdom (i.e., the world) to the good of His "special" kingdom (i.e., the church). The Westminster divines agree: "As the providence of God doth, in general, reach to all creatures, so, after a most special manner, it taketh care of his Church, and disposeth all things to the good thereof."[7]

The expression "all things" includes both prosperity and adversity. In the context of Romans 8:28, Paul is primarily concerned with adversity (or affliction). How God causes affliction to work for our good is difficult to understand. Flavel readily acknowledges that it "seems a very great paradox

---

5. Flavel, *Works*, VI:99; also see III:402.

6. Flavel, *Works*, IV:350. For Flavel's exposition of God's providence, see his treatise, *Divine Conduct; or, The Mystery of Providence: A Treatise upon Psalm 57:2*, in *Works*, IV:339–497.

7. *WCF*, V:VI. This is also reminiscent of Calvin (*Institutes*, I.XVII.1).

to most men, namely, that the afflictions of the saints can do them no hurt, and that the wisdom of men and angels cannot lay one circumstance of their condition (how uneasy so-ever it seems to be) better, or more to their advantage than God hath laid it."[8] As a solution to this "very great paradox," he simply points to God.[9] As the *WCF* affirms, God "is infinite in being and perfection, a most pure spirit, invisible, without body, parts, or passions; immutable, immense, eternal, incomprehensible, almighty, most wise, most holy, most free, most absolute."[10] In a word, God is sovereign; therefore, His control is absolute. God is immutable; therefore, His will is certain. God is mighty; therefore, His power is limitless. God is most wise; therefore, His plan is perfect. God is incomprehensible; therefore, His providence is inscrutable.[11] With this God before them, believers—while not always understanding His ways—are certain He causes all things to work together for their good.

This implies that believers are never in the grip of blind forces. On the contrary, everything that happens to them is divinely planned. This is a source of great comfort and

---

8. Flavel, *Works*, VI:83. For Flavel, the expression "all things" even includes sin: "God knows how to serve his own ends by the very sins of men, and yet have no communion at all in the sin he so over-rules. If a man let a dog out of his hand in pursuit of a hare, the dog hunts merely for a prey; but he that lets him go, uses the sagacity and nimbleness of the dog to serve his own ends by it" (*Works*, I:289).

9. For a brief treatment of the mystery of God's providence in the context of the current debate surrounding open theism, see J. S. Yuille, "How Pastoral is Open Theism? A Critique from the Writings of George Swinnock and Stephen Charnock," *Themelios* 32 (2007): 46-61. Flavel's understanding of God's providence approximates that of Swinnock and Charnock.

10. *WCF*, II:I.

11. Derek Thomas points to "God's incomprehensibility" as Calvin's interpretive key for understanding God's providence (*Proclaiming the Incomprehensible God: Calvin's Teaching on Job* [Ross-shire: Christian Focus, 2004], 17). For Calvin, see *Institutes*, I.V.1; I.XIII.21.

contentment. As Calvin puts it, the believer's "solace is to know his Heavenly Father so holds all things in his power, so rules by his authority and will, so governs by his wisdom, that nothing can befall except he determine it."[12]

God's Purpose

Second, we must embrace God's purpose. According to Flavel, it is twofold. First, God desires to manifest His glory by "clearing up the righteousness of his ways in the sufferings of his own people,"[13] and by manifesting "his power in their support, and his wisdom in the marvelous ways of their escape and deliverance."[14] Second, God desires to promote His people's happiness. He does so in five ways. (1) God uses suffering "to mortify the corruptions that are in their hearts." "There are," says Flavel, "rank weeds springing up in the best soil, which need such winter weather to rot them."[15] Likewise, our "corruptions" require affliction to drive them out. Thomas Watson concurs, "There is much corruption in the best heart; affliction does by degrees work it out, as the fire works out the dross from the gold."[16] (2) God uses suffering to produce "sincerity...to the joy and satisfaction of their own hearts."[17] When we persevere in affliction, God proves our faithfulness. This, in turn, is a great comfort as it confirms the sincerity of our faith. (3) God uses suffering to free the church from an "abundance of hypocrites, which were its reproach, as well as burden."[18] (4) God uses suffering to produce unity in the church: "to endear them to each

---

12. Calvin, *Institutes*, I.XVII.11; also see I.XVI.3.

13. Flavel, *Works*, VI:9.

14. Flavel, *Works*, VI:10.

15. Flavel, *Works*, VI:10; also see V:251.

16. Thomas Watson, *All Things for Good; or, A Divine Cordial* (1663; rpt., Edinburgh: Banner of Truth, 1994), 29.

17. Flavel, *Works*, VI:11.

18. Flavel, *Works*, VI:11.

other."[19] Affliction humbles us for our pride and bitterness. This, in turn, facilitates peace among God's people. (5) God uses suffering to awaken us to our duties: "to pray more frequently, spiritually, and fervently."[20] Simply put, prosperity spawns apathy and formality, but affliction cures us of both.

These five "uses" have a common purpose, namely, to bring us closer to God. There is no greater joy for the believer than fellowship with his God. And that is how God promotes His people's happiness through suffering. Watson agrees, stating, "The moon in the full is furthest off from the sun: so are many further off from God in the full-moon of prosperity.... The magnet of mercy does not draw us so near to God as the cords of affliction.... Thus affliction makes us happy, in bringing us nearer to God."[21]

God's Love

Third, we must embrace God's love. According to Flavel, we do so by remembering that we will "never be separated from Christ."[22] This confidence is based upon six "grounds."[23]

The first is "God's eternal electing love."[24] Flavel affirms that God chose us before the foundation of the world and,

---

19. Flavel, *Works*, VI:11.

20. Flavel, *Works*, VI:11.

21. Watson, *All Things for Good*, 31.

22. Flavel, *Works*, VI:79.

23. Also see *The Righteous Man's Refuge*, in which Flavel appeals to six chambers, which provide comfort in the midst of affliction: God's power, wisdom, faithfulness, unchangeableness, care, and love (*Works*, III:344-97). In this section, I also make reference to Flavel's discourse, entitled, "The Balm of the Covenant Applied to the Bleeding Wounds of Afflicted Saints," in *Works*, VI:83-119. It was originally delivered as a funeral sermon for Mr. John Upton.

24. Flavel, *Works*, VI:80. Elsewhere, Flavel writes, "The Scripture tells us, that from all eternity God hath chosen a certain number in Christ Jesus, to eternal life, and to the means by which they shall attain it, out of his mere good pleasure, and for the praise of his grace" (*Works*, II:571). He goes on to mention eight details: (1) It is an eter-

therefore, His decision was not based upon any "mutable ground or reason" in us, but upon His "immutable purpose."[25] The implication is this: God's love is unchangeable. As Paul makes clear, "For whom he did foreknow, he also did predestinate to be conformed to the image of his Son, that he might be the firstborn among many brethren. Moreover whom he did predestinate, them he also called: and whom he called, them he also justified: and whom he justified, them he also glorified" (Rom. 8:29-30).

The second "ground" is "the covenant of grace."[26] Flavel gives three reasons why this covenant confirms God's love for us. (1) The author of the covenant is not a "fickle creature," but a "faithful God." Therefore, as Paul says, "The gifts and the calling of God are irrevocable" (Rom. 11:29). (2) The blood of the covenant possesses "everlasting merit and efficacy." Therefore, God remembers our sins "no more" (Heb. 8:12). (3) The fulfillment of the covenant depends upon God, not man. Therefore, God provides what He requires of us; that is, faith. As Flavel puts it, "What is a condition in one scripture, is the matter of a promise in another."

The third "ground" is the believer's mystical union with Christ. Because of this union, it is "impossible" that we should be lost.[27] Flavel gives three reasons why. (1) "This union with his person brings interest in his properties along with it. Whatever he is, or hath, is for thee: his eye of knowledge, arm of power, bowels of pity, it is all for thee." (2) "This union with his person, secures thy feeble graces from perish-

---

nal act of God (Eph. 1:4). (2) It is immutable (2 Tim. 2:19). (3) It is in Christ (Eph. 1:4). (4) It is of a certain number of persons (John 17:2,6). (5) It is unto salvation as its end (1 Thess. 5:9). (6) It is unto sanctification as its means (2 Thess. 2:13-14). (7) It is according to God's good pleasure (Eph. 1:9). (8) It is for the praise of God's glorious grace (Eph. 1:5-6).

25. Flavel, *Works*, VI:80.

26. Flavel, *Works*, VI:80; also see II:56, VI:108-19.

27. Flavel, *Works*, VI:80.

ing (John 4:14). Thy grace has an everlasting spring. Whilst there is sap in this root, it will ascend into the branches." (3) "By this union thou becomest an integral part of Christ's body, which would be mutilated and defective, should thou be cut off and lost."

The fourth "ground" is Christ's "prevalent intercession."[28] Flavel encourages his readers to bear two questions in mind. (1) Who is it that intercedes for us? "It is Christ, whose person is most dear and ingratiated with the Father (John 11:42)." (2) What does Christ request? "Surely for nothing but what is most suitable to his Father's will." Therefore, when Christ prays, "Father, I will that they also, whom thou hast given me, be with me where I am; that they may behold my glory, which thou hast given me" (John 17:24), there is no doubt as to the Father's response.

The fifth "ground" is the presence of the Holy Spirit.[29] Paul says that we have received the "first fruits of the Spirit" (Rom. 8:23). We did so when we received the "Spirit of adoption" (Rom. 8:15). At that time, God placed us permanently in His family with all the rights and privileges of that family. The Holy Spirit, therefore, is a guarantee that we are heirs of God. As Flavel says, the Holy Spirit is "a seal, pledge, and earnest of the whole (Rom. 8:23; 2 Cor. 1:22)."

The sixth "ground" is Scripture.[30] Flavel speaks of "assertory" Scriptures such as John 6:39, where Christ says, "And this is the Father's will which hath sent me, that of all which he hath given me I should lose nothing, but should raise it up again at the last day."[31] Flavel also speaks of "promissory" Scriptures such as 1 Corinthians 1:8, where Paul affirms that Christ "shall also confirm you unto the end, that ye may

---

28. Flavel, *Works*, VI:80. For Flavel's thoughts on Christ's compassion as our high priest, see *Works*, II:46.

29. Flavel, *Works*, VI:80.

30. Flavel, *Works*, VI:81.

31. Also see John 10:28; 1 John 2:19.

be blameless in the day of our Lord Jesus Christ."[32] Lastly, Flavel speaks of "comparative" Scriptures such as Psalm 125:1, where the psalmist declares, "They that trust in the LORD shall be as Mount Zion, which cannot be removed, but abideth for ever."[33]

Each of the above "grounds" confirms God's love for us. Therefore, in the midst of suffering, we are convinced that there is nothing that can "separate us from the love of God, which is in Christ Jesus our Lord" (Rom. 8:39).

Conclusion

To these three truths (God's promise, God's purpose, and God's love), Flavel adds the wondrous truth that Christ Himself shares in our suffering. There is an intimate relationship between Christ and His mystical body whereby our suffering is His suffering. In Flavel's estimation, this is a cause of wonder:

> We do not only partake of what is his, but he partakes of what is ours: he hath fellowship with us in all our wants, sorrows, miseries and afflictions; and we have communion with him in his righteousness, grace, sonship and glory: he partakes of our misery, and we partake of his blessedness; our sufferings are his sufferings (Col. 1:24). O, what an honour is it to thee, poor wretch, to whom a great many would not turn aside to ask how thou dost; to have a King, yea, the prince of all the kings of the earth, to pity, relieve, sympathize, groan and bleed with thee, to sit by thee in all thy troubles, and give thee his cordials; to say thy troubles are my troubles, and thy afflictions are my afflictions: whatever toucheth thee, toucheth me also. O what name shall we give unto such grace as this?[34]

---

32. Also see Isa. 54:10; Jer. 32:40.

33. Also see Ps. 1:3; 1 John 4:14.

34. Flavel, *Works*, II:151.

Chapter 9

—— ⋅⟨∘⟩⋅ ——

THE JOY OF UNION
WITH CHRIST

By virtue of our union with Christ, we receive His spiritual blessings (chapter five), bear His fruit (chapter six), partake of His sanctifying Spirit (chapter seven), and fill up what is lacking in His afflictions (chapter eight). In addition, we experience communion with God. With this, we arrive at the heart of Flavel's doctrine of the believer's mystical union with Christ.[1] Christ declares, "Behold, I stand at the door, and knock: if any man hear my voice, and open the door, I will come in to him, and will sup with him, and he with me" (Rev. 3:20). In this verse, Flavel sees union between Christ and the believer: "I will come in to him, and will sup with him." And he sees communion between the believer and Christ: "and he with me."

The Nature of Communion with God

Flavel believes that the nature of this communion is "found to lie in a spiritual correspondency betwixt Christ and the soul. God lets forth influences upon our souls, and we, by the assistance of his Spirit, make returns again unto God."[2] John Owen[3] provides a similar definition, stating, "Our com-

---

1. Many of the insights in this chapter are gleaned from Flavel's treatise, *England's Duty Under the Present Gospel Liberty (1689)*, in *Works*, IV:3-267. It consists of eleven sermons, based upon Rev. 3:20.

2. Flavel, *Works*, IV:240; also see IV:436.

3. John Owen (1616-1683) was a Puritan divine of Independent convictions. He became vice-chancellor at Oxford in 1652.

munion, then, with God consisteth in his communication of himself unto us, with our returnal unto him of that which he requireth and accepteth, flowing from that union which in Jesus Christ we have with him."[4] These definitions raise an obvious question: When does God let forth His "influences" upon our souls (i.e., communicate Himself to us) so that we make "returns" to Him? Flavel identifies three instances in which such communion takes place.

First, there is communion with God *"in the contemplation of the Divine attributes*, and the impressions God makes by them upon our souls, whilst we meditate on them."[5] Flavel provides six examples. (1) God impresses His "immense greatness" upon us, thereby making "an awful, humbling impression upon the soul." "When I consider," says Flavel, "what a great God the Creator of the world is, I am justly astonished that ever he should set his heart upon so vile a thing as man." (2) God impresses His "purity and holiness" upon us, thereby producing "shame and deep abasement in the soul." Flavel appeals to the examples of Isaiah and Job, who were both overwhelmed by God's holiness and, as a result, were acutely aware of their own sinfulness.[6] (3) God impresses His "goodness and mercy" upon us, thereby working "an ingenuous thaw and melting of the heart." His goodness is evident in "external providences" and "spiritual mercies." (4) God impresses His "veracity and faithfulness" upon us,

---

4. Owen, *Works*, II:8-9. In his treatise *Of Communion with God*, Owen considers the Christian's communion with the Father in love, with the Son in grace, and with the Spirit in consolation. He comments, "The way and means, then, on the part of the saints, whereby in Christ they enjoy communion with God, are all the spiritual and holy actings and outgoings of their souls in those graces, and by those ways, wherein both the moral and instituted worship of God doth consist. Faith, love, trust, joy, etc., are the natural or moral worship of God, whereby those in whom they are have communion with him" (*Works*, II:11).

5. Flavel, *Works*, IV:240.

6. See Isa. 6:3-5; Job 40:4-5.

thereby begetting "trust and holy confidence." His faithfulness is seen in His word and providence. (5) God impresses His "anger and displeasure" upon us, thereby resulting in repentance. "Shame and blushing," says Flavel, "are as excellent signs of communion with God as the sweetest smiles." (6) God impresses His "omniscience" upon us, thereby producing sincerity. Turning to the example of David, Flavel observes, "The consideration that he was always before the eye of God was his preservative from iniquity, yea, from his own iniquity." [7]

Second, there is communion with God "in the exercises of our graces in the various duties of religion; in praying, hearing, sacraments, &c. in all which the Spirit of the Lord influences the graces of his people, and they return the fruits thereof in some measure to him. As God hath planted various graces in regenerate souls, so he hath appointed various duties to exercise and draw forth those graces; and when they do so, then have his people sweet actual communion with him." [8] We will consider the use of these duties in the next chapter. For our present discussion, it is enough to highlight four examples of the "graces" that are exercised in duties. (1) There is the grace of repentance: "The soul pours out itself before the Lord with much bitterness and brokenness of heart." (2) There is the grace of faith: "They find from the Lord inward support, rest, and refreshment." (3) There is the grace of love: "The strength of the soul is drawn forth to Christ in love, and this the Lord repays in kind, love for love." (4) There is the grace of passive obedience: "Christians are enabled to exercise their patience, meekness, and longsuffering for Christ, in return to which, the Lord gives them the singular consolations of his Spirit, double returns of joy." [9]

7. Flavel, *Works*, IV:240-43.

8. Flavel, *Works*, IV:244.

9. Flavel, *Works*, IV:244-45.

Third, there is communion with God "in the way of his providences."[10] As Flavel explains, "The Lord chastens his children…in answer whereunto gracious souls return meek and child-like submission, a fruit of the Spirit of adoption.… When this produces trust in God, and resignation to the pleasure of his will, here is communion with God in times of distress and difficulty."[11]

In each of the above instances, God communicates Himself to our souls so that we make "returns" to Him.[12]

---

10. Flavel, *Works*, IV:245.

11. Flavel, *Works*, IV:245.

12. For Flavel, this is at the heart of what it means to fear God. See *A Practical Treatise of Fear, Works*, III:239-320. "This fear," he explains, "is a gracious habit or principle planted by God in the soul, whereby the soul is kept under an holy awe of the eye of God, and from thence is inclined to perform and do what pleaseth him, and to shun and avoid whatsoever he forbids and hates" (*Works*, III:252). For the sake of clarity, it is important to distinguish between ungodly (servile) fear and godly (filial) fear. As Flavel notes, "There is a fear which is the effect of sin springing from guilt, and hurrying the soul into more guilt; and there is a fear which is the effect of grace, springing from our love to God, and his interest, and driving the soul to God in the way of duty" (*Works*, III:242). The difference between the two is determined by one's view of God. Ungodly fear is the result of viewing God as a potential source of harm. It causes people to take steps to minimize the perceived threat while remaining steadfast in their sin. In marked contrast, godly fear is the result of viewing God as the greatest good. According to Brian Gerrish, Calvin distinguishes two types of fear: "a merely servile dread of God and the reverence for God that fits those who are *both* servants *and* children. The difference between the two types is plain from the fact that whereas those who lack piety (the *impii*) are frightened by the thought of divine vengeance, *fidelium timor* is fear, not of punishment, but of giving offense to the heavenly father" (*Grace and Gratitude: The Eucharist Theology of John Calvin* [Minneapolis: Fortress Press, 1993], 67, n. 71). See Calvin, *Institutes*, III.II.26-27. According to John Murray, there is the fear that consists in being afraid. It elicits anguish and terror. There is also the fear of reverence. It elicits confidence and love (*Principles of Conduct* [Grand Rapids: Eerdmans, 1957], 233). He adds that the fear of God in us is that frame of heart

These returns include the stirring of the affections: love, desire, delight, fear, sorrow, trust, and hope. For Flavel, these affections "are the strong and sensible motions" of the soul by which it is "capable of union with the highest good." When these affections are directed toward God, the soul rests in Him as its center.[13] And this is communion with God.

Flavel turns to the Song of Solomon (or Canticles) for language to express these "returns unto God." In typical Puritan fashion, he interprets this book as a spiritual allegory, depicting the relationship between Christ and the church.[14] It is, he says, "a spiritual *epithalamium*, sung in parts betwixt the heavenly bridegroom and the bride. The matter of it is most spiritual and weighty, the style of it rapturous and lofty, the intimate union and communion of Christ and the

---

and mind that reflects our apprehension of who and what God is, and this leads to total commitment to Him (*Principles of Conduct*, 242).

13. Flavel, *Works*, II:524; also see II:510.

14. Flavel, *Works*, VI:450. Similarly, in reference to Psalm 45:7, Flavel writes, "The words read, are a part of the excellent *song of love*, that heavenly *Epithalamium*, wherein the spiritual espousals of Christ and the church are figuratively and very elegantly celebrated and shadowed. The subject matter of this psalm is the very same with the whole book of the Canticles; and in this psalm, under the figure of king Solomon, and the daughter of Egypt, whom he espoused, the spiritual espousals of Christ and the church are set forth and represented to us" (*Works*, II:141). Allegorical interpretation among the Puritans is the subject of some controversy. Paul Jewett makes a helpful distinction by noting that allegorical interpretation is not the same as the interpretation of allegories. Rather, it is concerned with interpreting a text in terms of something else. According to Jewett, there is a "rational" basis for such allegorizing as long as it "presupposes the unity and continuity of biblical revelation." After all, the NT authors interpret the OT in terms of Jesus' work. In so doing, however, they never undermine the historicity of the original texts. That is the test ("Concerning the Allegorical Interpretation of Scripture," *Westminster Theological Journal* 17 [1954]: 1-20). For Owen's use of Song of Solomon, see Ferguson, *John Owen on the Christian Life*, 78-86. Of particular note is Ferguson's comment that "the Song of Solomon is for *Owen* a transcript of the affections of Christian experience" (*John Owen on the Christian Life*, 78).

church."[15] In it, the bride (church) expresses her "conjugal affections" for the bridegroom (Christ)—the principal affections being desire and delight.

The Church's Desire for Christ

By way of definition, Edward Reynolds describes "desire" as "the wing of the soule whereby it moveth, and is carried to the thing which it loveth...to feed it selfe upon it, and to be satisfied with it."[16] In terms of the church's desire for Christ, Flavel turns to Song of Solomon 3:1-5. These verses depict the "value of the divine presence with the soul,"[17] in that the bridegroom has departed, but the bride is not content to let him go. Therefore, she searches for him. Flavel maintains that believers are likewise "sensible of God's recesses, and withdrawment from their spirits; they feel how the ebb follows the flood, and how the waters abate."[18] When they perceive His absence, they immediately set about searching for Him: "God goes off from your souls, but you cannot go

---

15. Flavel, *Works*, VI:547. Owen sees this relationship expressed in Song 2:4-7. It bears four marks. (1) There is sweetness, as suggested by the banquet hall: "The grace exhibited by Christ in his ordinances is refreshing, strengthening, comforting, and full of sweetness to the souls of the saints." (2) There is delight, as suggested by the bride's words: "I am lovesick." "Upon the discovery," writes Owen, "of the excellency and sweetness of Christ in the banqueting house, the soul is instantly overpowered, and cries out to be made partaker of the fullness of it." (3) There is safety, as suggested by the banner: "Christ hath a banner for his saints; and that is love. All their protection is from his love; and they shall have all the protection his love can give them." (4) There is support and consolation, as suggested by the two hands: "'The hand under the head,' is supportment, sustaining grace, in pressures and difficulties; and 'the hand that doth embrace,' the hand upon the heart is joy and consolation" (*Works*, II:44-45).

16. Edward Reynolds, *A Treatise of the Passions and Faculties of the Soul* (London, 1640), 161.

17. Flavel, *Works*, I:411, 415; also see V:571, VI:37. This desire is also depicted in Song 5:2-8. See II:366; VI:389.

18. Flavel, *Works*, VI:389.

off from him. No, your hearts are mourning after the Lord, seeking him carefully with tears: complaining of his absence, as the greatest evil in this world."[19] Owen expresses a similar sentiment:

> The soul finding not Christ present in his *wonted* manner, *warming, cherishing, reviving it* with love, nigh to it, supping with it, always filling its thoughts with himself, dropping myrrh and sweet tastes of love into it; but, on the contrary, that other thoughts crowd in and perplex the heart, and Christ is not nigh when inquired after; it presently inquires into the cause of all this, calls itself to an account what it hath *done*, how it hath *behaved itself*, that it is not with it as at other times.[20]

Because of her longing, the bride enters the streets to search for her beloved. Finally, she finds him. In a similar fashion, the believer desires Christ in His absence and, therefore, seeks after Him. Having found Him, "the soul lays fast hold on him by faith...refuses to part with him any more, in vehemency of love."[21]

The Church's Delight in Christ

Again, by way of definition, Reynolds describes delight as "nothing else but the Sabbath of our thoughts, and that sweet tranquility of mind, which we receive from the Presence and Fruition of that good, whereunto our Desires have carried us."[22] For the church's delight in Christ, Flavel turns to Song of Solomon 5:9-16. In verse 9, the daughters of Jerusalem ask, "What is thy beloved more than another beloved?" The

---

19. Flavel, *Works*, I:415.

20. Owen, *Works*, II:129.

21. Owen, *Works*, II:131-32.

22. Reynolds, *Passions and Faculties*, 199. For the place of joy among the Puritans, see J. Gwyn-Thomas, "The Puritan Doctrine of Christian Joy" in *Puritan Papers: Vol. II*, ed. J. I. Packer (Phillipsburg: Presbyterian and Reformed, 2001), 119-240.

bride's response, in verses 10-16,[23] culminates in her declaration: "*He is altogether lovely.*" Flavel applies these words to Christ, stating, "Look on him in what respect or particular you will; cast your eye upon this lovely object, and view him any way; turn him in your serious thoughts which way you will; consider his person, his offices, his works, or any other thing belonging to him; you will find him altogether lovely."[24]

Flavel proceeds to do just that. (1) Christ is altogether lovely in His person: "The wonderful union and perfection of the divine and human nature in Christ, render him an object of admiration and adoration to angels and men."[25] (2) Christ is altogether lovely in His offices: "All the promises of illumination, counsel and direction flow out of the *prophetical office*; all the promises of reconciliation, peace, pardon, and acceptation flow out of the *priestly office*…all the promises of converting, increasing, defending, directing, and supplying grace, flow out of the *kingly office*."[26] (3) Christ is altogether lovely in His relations. As Redeemer, He delivers us from the depths of misery.[27] As Bridegroom, He espouses us to Himself—we who are "deformed, defiled, and altogether unworthy."[28] As Advocate, He "pleads the cause of believers in heaven; appears for them in the presence of God, to prevent all new breaches, and continues the state of friendship and peace betwixt God and us."[29] As Friend, He loves us with a "fervent and strong affection."[30]

---

23. For Owen's exposition of these verses, see *Works*, II:49-78. For Pearse, see *Best Match*, 56-70.

24. Flavel, *Works*, II:215.

25. Flavel, *Works*, II:218.

26. Flavel, *Works*, II:219.

27. Flavel, *Works*, II:219.

28. Flavel, *Works*, II:220.

29. Flavel, *Works*, II:221.

30. Flavel, *Works*, II:222.

Christ's loveliness in His person, works, and offices causes the believer to cry with delight: "This is my beloved, and this is my friend, O daughters of Jerusalem" (Song 5:16).[31] Flavel defines such spiritual delight as "the complacency and well-pleasedness of a renewed heart, in conversing with God, and the things of God, resulting from the agreeableness of them to the spiritual temper of his mind."[32] He breaks this down into four components. (1) The "nature" of delight is the "complacency, rest, and satisfaction of the mind in God and spiritual things." (2) The "object" of delight is "God himself, and the things which relate to him." (3) The "subject" of delight is "a renewed heart." (4) The "principle" of delight is "the agreeableness of spiritual things to the temper and frame of a renewed mind." All told, the soul's "spiritual senses" are satisfied in God.

Conclusion

These two "conjugal affections"—desire and delight—are the principal "returns" made by the soul unto God once He lets forth His "influences" upon it. And this, for Flavel, is the essence of the soul's communion with God—"the life of our life, the joy of our hearts; a heaven upon earth."[33] It is "a felt

---

31. How is this delight manifested? Owen replies: (1) "By her exceeding great care to keep his company and society, when once she had obtained it." (2) "By the utmost impatience of his absence, with desires still of nearer communion with him." Owen calls this "a holy greediness of delight." (3) "By her solicitousness, trouble, and perplexity, in his loss and withdrawings." In other words, "whenever Christ is absent, it is night with a believer" (*Works*, II:125-28).

32. Flavel, *Works*, II:409.

33. Flavel, *Works*, IV:250. Flavel describes communion by way of twenty "excellencies." (1) "It is the *assimilating* instrument whereby the soul is…fashioned after the image of God." (2) "It is the *beauty* of the soul, in the eyes of God and all good men." (3) "It is the *centre* which rests the motions of a weary soul." (4) "It is the *desire* of all gracious souls." (5) "It is the *delight* of all the children of God." (6) "It is the *envy* of Satan." (7) "It is the *end* of all ordinances."

presence of God which no words can make another to understand; they feel that fountain flowing abundantly into the dry pits, the heart fills apace, the empty thoughts swell with a fullness of spiritual things, which strive for vent."[34]

---

(8) "It is the *evidence* of our union with Christ." (9) "It is *ease* in all pains, sweet and sensible ease to a troubled soul." (10) "It is *food* to the soul, and the most delicious, pleasant, proper, and satisfying food that ever it tasted." (11) "It is the *guard* of the soul against the assaults of temptation." (12) "It is the *honour* of the soul, and the greatest honour that ever God conferred on any creature." (13) "It is the *instrument* of mortification." (14) "It is the *kernel* of all duties and ordinances." (15) "It is the *light* of the soul in darkness." (16) "It is *liberty* to the straitened soul, and the most comfortable and excellent liberty in the whole world." (17) "It is a *mercy* purchased by the blood of Christ for believers." (18) "It is *natural* to the new creature; the inclination and instinct of the new creature leadeth to communion with God." (19) "It is the *occupation* and trade of all sanctified persons." (20) "It is *oil* to the wheels of obedience, which makes the soul go on cheerfully in the ways of the Lord" (*Works*, IV:250-59).

34. Flavel, *Works*, VI:389. For Flavel on spiritual ecstasies, see *Works*, III:54-56, where he divides them into two categories: (1) "Extraordinary," where the soul may be caught up from the body (e.g., Paul in 2 Cor. 12:2-3); or, the body may be elevated above its natural ability (e.g., Stephen in Acts 7:55-56). (2) "Ordinary," being foretastes of heaven "come into the heart, upon the steady and more fixed views of the world to come, by faith, and the more raised spiritual actings of grace in duty."

Chapter 10

---•◦•---

THE PRACTICE OF UNION
WITH CHRIST

How does the believer cultivate communion with God? As mentioned in the previous chapter, the answer is found in spiritual duties. Flavel affirms that God has appointed "so many ordinances and duties of religion, on purpose to maintain daily communion betwixt Christ and his people."[1] Flavel's commitment to these "duties of religion" arises from his conviction that the Holy Spirit uses them to let forth God's "influences" upon the soul so that we make suitable "returns" to Him. He speaks of numerous private and public duties, but five emerge to the forefront.

Watching

The first is watching. Flavel asserts that there are various encumbrances that inhibit communion with God.[2] We are, for example, distracted by "worldly employments," deadened by

---

1. Flavel, *Works*, IV:247. Again, "There is pure and sincere milk in the breasts of ordinances; a believer sucks the very breasts of Christ in hid duties and doth grow thereby (1 Pet. 2:2). They do grow more and more judicious, experienced, humble, mortified, and heavenly, by conversing with the Lord so frequently in his appointments" (*Works*, V:572). Don Whitney provides a modern-day perspective of the Puritan understanding of spiritual duties (or means of grace), explaining that they are "like channels of God's transforming grace. As we place ourselves in them to seek communion with Christ, his grace flows to us and we are changed" (*Spiritual Disciplines for the Christian Life* [Colorado Springs: NavPress, 1991], 18-19).

2. Flavel, *Works*, IV:261.

"formality," pestered by "temptations," hardened by "inward decay of love," and impoverished by "spiritual pride." For this reason, we must keep "watch" over our souls.[3] According to Flavel, we do so by performing six "acts": (1) "frequent observation of the frame of the heart, turning in and examining how the case stands with it"; (2) "deep humiliation for heart-evils and disorders"; (3) "earnest supplications and instant prayer for heart-purifying and rectifying grace, when sin hath defiled and disordered it"; (4) "the imposing of strong engagements and bonds upon ourselves to walk more accurately with God, and avoid occasions whereby the heart may be induced to sin"; (5) "a constant holy jealousy over our own hearts"; and (6) "the realizing of God's presence with us." [4]

Keeping watch over the soul is foundational to other spiritual duties, because their effectiveness depends in large part upon the removal of those encumbrances that dampen the affections. Unconfessed sin, unchecked pride, and undisciplined thoughts tend to render the soul insensible to any "influences" that God sets forth in duties. Our first responsibility, therefore, is to remove all hindrances to communion.

Listening

In a state of watchfulness, the soul is ready to pursue God in other duties. Flavel views our attendance upon the preaching of God's Word as the most important of these. Richard Baxter[5] agrees:

---

3. Flavel deals extensively with this subject in *A Saint Indeed; or, The Great Work of a Christian Explained and Applied*, *Works*, V:417-508. For twelve "special seasons" when such watchfulness is particularly required, see *Works*, V:437-90.

4. Flavel, *Works*, V:426-28.

5. Richard Baxter (1615-1691) was a Presbyterian divine, who ministered at Kidderminster. He was ejected from the Church of England for Nonconformity in 1662.

The *reading* of the word of God, and the explication and application of it in good books, is a means to possess the mind with sound, orderly, and working apprehensions of God, and of his holy truths: so that in such reading our understandings are oft illuminated with a heavenly light, and our hearts are touched with a special delightful relish of that truth; and they are secretly attracted and engaged unto God and all the powers of our souls are excited and animated to a holy obedient life. The same word *preached*…hath a greater advantage for the same illumination and excitement of the soul.[6]

This view of preaching as the most effective spiritual duty stems from Calvin's concept of the "sacramental word."[7] Regarding Romans 10:17,[8] Calvin comments, "This is a remarkable passage with regard to the efficacy of preaching; for he [i.e., Paul] testifies that by it faith is produced…. When it pleases the Lord to work, it becomes the instrument of his power."[9] Brian Gerrish explains Calvin's thought as follows: "The word is not simply information about God; it is the instrument through which union with Christ is effected and his grace imparted."[10] Howard Hageman agrees, "For Calvin the reading and preaching of the Word is the way in which Christ comes to us and shares himself with us…. Because the Word is the instrument through which Christ is given to

---

6. Richard Baxter, *The Divine Life* in *The Practical Works of Richard Baxter: Select Treatises* (London: Blackie & Son, 1863; rpt., Grand Rapids: Baker Book House, 1981), 195. My italics.

7. Calvin, *Institutes*, IV.XIV.4.

8. "So then faith cometh by hearing, and hearing by the word of God."

9. John Calvin, *Commentaries on the Epistle of the Apostle Paul to the Romans* in *Calvin's Commentaries* (Grand Rapids: Baker Books, 2003), XIX:401.

10. Gerrish, *Grace and Gratitude*, 76.

us, it stands at the very centre of the life of the Church and at the very centre of the life and growth of the Christian."[11]

Like Calvin, Flavel believes that preaching is the principal means by which God communicates Himself to the soul. Because of this, we must be careful in our approach to it.[12] He mentions two "antecedents."[13] First, we must prepare ourselves by (1) considering "the greatness and holiness of that God whom we approach in hearing the word," (2) "discharging" our "heart from worldly cares," and (3) "longing after the word for further communications of grace by it." Second, we must pray, requesting that God (1) assist the preacher, and (2) pour out His Spirit with the Word. As for "concomitants" to preaching, we must exercise (1) "an assenting act of faith" whereby we acknowledge the Word's "divine authority," and (2) "an applying act of faith" whereby we take to heart what is proclaimed.[14] Finally, in terms of "subsequents" to preaching,[15] we must (1) preserve what is proclaimed "in our hearts and memories," and (2) produce "the fruits of it in our lives."

Meditating

Closely related to listening is meditating. Flavel places tremendous importance upon this spiritual duty.[16] The reason

---

11. Hageman, "Reformed Spirituality," 66.

12. Peter Lewis considers the Puritans' approach to the Word preached under three headings: (1) preparation for hearing; (2) behavior necessary when hearing; and (3) duties after hearing (*Genius of Puritanism*, 53-59).

13. Flavel, *Works*, VI:272-73.

14. Flavel, *Works*, VI:274.

15. Flavel, *Works*, VI:275.

16. For Flavel's view of the relationship between meditation and mortification, see *Works*, II:391-94. For his meditations upon God's providence, see *Works*, IV:413-96. For his meditations in preparation for the Lord's Supper, see *Twelve Sacramental Meditations upon Select Places of Scripture*, in *Works*, VI:378-459. For his meditations upon nature, see *Husbandry Spiritualized: The Heavenly Use of Earthly Things*, in

for this stems from his view of the understanding as the primary faculty of the soul.[17] He writes, "Light in the mind is necessarily antecedent to the sweet and heavenly motions and elevations of the affections."[18] In short, the affections cannot love what the understanding does not know. The believer's greatest duty, therefore, is to cultivate a "sensible" or "practical" knowledge of God; that is, a knowledge that has its "seat in the heart."[19] Flavel explains:

> Knowledge is man's excellency above the beasts that perish (Ps. 32:9). The knowledge of Christ is the Christian's excellency above the Heathen (1 Cor. 1:23-24). Practical and saving knowledge of Christ is the sincere Christian's excellency above the self-cozening hypocrite (Heb. 6:4,6). But methodical and well-digested knowledge of Christ is the strong Christian's excellency above the weak (Heb. 5:12-14). A saving, though an immethodical knowledge of Christ, will bring us to heaven (John 17:2), but a regular and methodical, as well as a saving knowledge of him, will bring heaven into us (Col. 2:2-3).[20]

This "methodical and well-digested knowledge" is the product of meditation, which J. I. Packer describes as:

> an activity of holy thought, consciously performed in the presence of God, under the eye of God, by the help of God, as a means of communion with God. Its purpose is to clear one's mental and spiritual vision of God, and to let His truth make its full and proper impact on one's mind and heart.... Its effect is ever to humble us, as we contemplate God's greatness and glory, and our own littleness and sinfulness, and

---

Works, V:3-205; and *Navigation Spiritualized: A New Compass for Seamen*, in *Works*, V:206-92.

17. Flavel, *Works*, II:503.
18. Flavel, *Works*, I:131.
19. Flavel, *Works*, I:131.
20. Flavel, *Works*, I:21.

to encourage and reassure us ... as we contemplate the unsearchable riches of divine mercy displayed in the Lord Jesus Christ.[21]

Here, Packer states that the purpose of meditation is to enable God's truth to "make its full and proper impact on one's mind and heart." In the context of Puritan meditation,[22] he describes this "impact" as follows:

Knowing themselves to be creatures of thought, affection, and will, and knowing that God's way to the human heart (the will) is via the human head (the mind), the Puritans practiced meditation, discursive and systematic, on the whole range of biblical truth as they saw it applying to themselves. Puritan meditation on Scripture was modeled on the Puritan sermon; in meditation the Puritan would seek to search and challenge his heart, stir his affections to hate sin and love righteousness, and encourage himself with God's promises, just as Puritan preachers would do from the pulpit.[23]

Once again, the Puritan predilection for the soul's faculties steps to the forefront. The goal of Puritan meditation is to apply Scripture successively to the faculties of understanding, affections, and will. Peter Toon states, "In meditation a channel is somehow opened between the mind, heart, and will—what the mind receives enters the heart and goes into

---

21. J. I. Packer, *Knowing God* (London: Hodder and Stoughton, 1975), 20.

22. For a brief overview of Puritan meditation, see Beeke, *Puritan Reformed Spirituality*, 73-100. For an extensive list of subjects for meditation, see 87-89. In Flavel's estimation, "There is no doctrine more excellent in itself, or more necessary to be preached and studied, than the doctrine of Jesus Christ, and him crucified" (*Works*, I:34). He adds, "As Christ is the door that opens heaven, so knowledge is the key that opens Christ" (*Works*, I:35).

23. Packer, *Quest for Godliness*, 24.

action via the will."[24] In terms of the affections specifically, he states, "Meditation was seen as a divinely appointed way of stimulating or raising the affections toward the glory of God."[25] All together then, meditation begins in the mind with serious thoughts of God. These thoughts stimulate "the affections toward the glory of God." In turn, the will goes "into action" based upon the affections.[26]

Praying

Following meditation is prayer: "an offering up of our desires unto God, for things agreeable to his will, in the name of Christ, with confession of our sins, and thankful acknowledgement of his service."[27] Having meditated upon Scripture, the soul is stirred to approach God in adoration, confession, and supplication. This stirring of the affections in prayer is, for Flavel, the height of communion with God. "Prayer is," says he, "amongst duties, as faith is amongst graces."[28]

While it is true that the Holy Spirit "excites the heart to pray," "suggests the matters of our prayers," and "stirreth up suitable affections in prayer," we can improve our prayers in "divers ways." By improvement, Flavel means that we can learn to pray with more "humility," "sincerity," "zeal," "readiness," and "faith."[29] We do so by (1) being frequent in prayer, (2) not grieving the Holy Spirit, (3) searching our hearts, and (4) looking more at the exercise of graces.[30] Furthermore,

---

24. Peter Toon, *From Mind to Heart: Christian Meditation Today* (Grand Rapids: Baker Books, 1987), 18.

25. Toon, *From Mind to Heart*, 94.

26. For a brief treatment of the methodology behind Puritan meditation, see J. S. Yuille, "Puritan Meditation: The Gateway from the Head to the Heart," *Eusebeia: The Bulletin of the Jonathan Edwards Centre for Reformed Spirituality* 4 (2005): 7-16.

27. Flavel, *Works*, VI:291. See *WSC*, Question 98.

28. Flavel, *Works*, VI:64.

29. Flavel, *Works*, VI:66.

30. Flavel, *Works*, VI:66-67.

we must give attention to the "matter" and "manner" of our prayers. As for the first, they must be agreeable to God's will.[31] As for the second, they must be sincere and fervent.[32]

Partaking of the Lord's Supper

Flavel's use of spiritual duties culminates in the Lord's Supper.[33] He believes that "it is a seal of the covenant of God in Christ, wherein, by certain outward signs, instituted by our Saviour, Christ and all his benefits are signified, conveyed, and sealed to the worthy receiver."[34] Again:

> This ordinance hath a direct and peculiar tendency to the improvement and strengthening of faith. It is a pledge superadded to the promise for faith's sake: Heavenly and sublime mysteries do therein stoop down to your senses, that you may have the clearer apprehensions of them; and the clearer the apprehensions are, the stronger the assent of faith must needs be: By this seal also the promise comes to be more ratified to us; and the firmer the promise appears to the soul, the more bold and adventurous faith is in casting itself upon it.[35]

Further to this, Flavel views the Lord's Supper as the place where Christ chooses to commune in a special way with His bride (the church). "It is," says he, "one of the strongest bonds of union betwixt them that can be."[36] This emphasis places Flavel in the vicinity of Calvin's view of the

---

31. See James 4:3; 1 John 5:14.

32. Flavel, *Works*, VI:292.

33. See Flavel's sermon "The second preparative Act of Christ for his own death," which is part of *The Fountain of Life*, in *Works*, I:259-70. This sermon is based upon 1 Cor. 11:23-25.

34. Flavel, *Works*, VI:464.

35. Flavel, *Works*, VI:45.

36. Flavel, *Works*, I:267.

sacrament.[37] For his part, Calvin makes it clear that the sacraments do not have any intrinsic value, affirming, "We must beware lest we…think that a hidden power is joined and fastened to the sacraments by which they of themselves confer the graces of the Holy Spirit upon us.… They are of no further benefit unless the Holy Spirit accompanies them. For it is he who opens our minds and hearts and makes us receptive to this testimony."[38] This last statement is crucial to Calvin's view of Christ's presence in the bread and wine. In his opinion, the Holy Spirit "nourishes faith spiritually through the sacraments."[39] This means that Christ gives spiritual nourishment from His glorified body through the Holy Spirit to those who partake of the Supper. Christ is not physically present in the bread and wine, because His glorified body is in heaven. However, Christ comes down to believers at His Supper through the Holy Spirit. For Calvin, therefore, the body and blood of Christ are truly present in the bread and wine. This means that when we partake of the Lord's Supper, we consume Christ spiritually.[40]

This is the tradition in which Flavel stands. In his treatise, *Sacramental Meditations Upon Divers Select Places of Scripture*,[41] he includes a sermon, based upon John 6:55, where Christ

---

37. When it comes to the Reformers, there are three main viewpoints concerning the nature of Christ's presence in the elements. They are usually identified with Luther, Zwingli, and Calvin. For a summary of the various views, see Brian Gerrish, "The Lord's Supper in the Reformed Confessions," *Theology Today* 23 (1966): 224-43.

38. Calvin, *Institutes*, IV.XIV.17.

39. Calvin, *Institutes*, IV.XIV.12.

40. See Calvin, *Institutes*, IV.XVII.12, 33. Joseph Tylenda demonstrates Calvin's preference for the word *true* as opposed to *real* in regard to Christ's presence in the Supper in "Calvin and Christ's Presence in the Supper – True or Real," *Scottish Journal of Theology* 27 (1974): 65-75. For Owen and the dynamic view, see Ferguson, *John Owen on the Christian Life*, 221-22.

41. Flavel, *Works*, VI:378-460. This treatise consists of twelve sacramental sermons.

declares, "For my flesh is meat indeed, and my blood is drink indeed." According to Flavel, Christ's flesh and blood resemble meat and drink in the following ways.[42] (1) Just as meat and drink are necessary to support physical life, Christ's flesh and blood are necessary to support spiritual life. (2) Just as meat and drink are "most sweet and desirable" to those that are physically hungry and thirsty, Christ's flesh and blood are "most sweet and desirable" to those who are spiritually hungry and thirsty. (3) Just as meat and drink must undergo an alteration before they nourish the body, Christ's flesh and blood must undergo an alteration before they nourish the soul. Simply put, "Christ must be ground betwixt the upper and nether millstone of the wrath of God, and malice of men." (4) Just as meat and drink must have a "natural union" with the body, Christ's flesh and blood must have a "spiritual union" with the soul. (5) Just as meat and drink must be taken regularly or else natural life will languish, Christ's flesh and blood must be taken regularly or else spiritual life will languish.

By the Holy Spirit, therefore, we commune with Christ in His Supper. "Among all those ordinances," writes Flavel, "wherein the blessed God manifests himself to the children of men, none are found to set forth more of the joy of his presence, than that of the Lord's Supper: at that blessed table, are such sensible embraces betwixt Christ and believers, as do afford delight and solace, beyond the joy of the whole earth."[43]

Conclusion

From the foregoing discussion, it is evident that—for Flavel —a diligent use of spiritual duties is essential for cultivating

---

42. Flavel, *Works*, VI:445-46.
43. Flavel, *Works*, VI:381.

communion with God.[44] "There is," Flavel says, "real communion betwixt God and his people in duties…God pours forth of his Spirit upon them, and they pour forth their hearts to God."[45] Again:

> Certainly, reader, there is a time when God comes nigh to men in duty, when he deals familiarly with men, and sensibly fills their souls with unusual powers and delights. The near approaches of God to their souls are felt by them, (for souls have their senses as well as bodies) and now are their minds abstracted and marvelously refined from all that is material and earthly, and swallowed up in spiritual excellencies and glories. These are the real prelibations, or foretastes of glory, which no man can by words, make another to understand, as he himself doth that feels them.[46]

For this reason, Flavel stresses the diligent use of duties: "You find in the word, a world of work cut out for Christians; there is hearing-work, praying-work, reading, meditating, and self-examining-work; it puts him also upon a constant watch over all the corruptions of his heart. Oh, what a world of work hath a Christian about him?"[47] Yet, while stressing human effort, Flavel is careful to note that the practice of duties must not be viewed as an end in itself. He explains that believers "have special regard to duties in point

---

44. This pursuit of spiritual duties is the essence of Flavel's spirituality. In this way, he falls in the tradition of Calvin. Hageman asks, "What was the spirituality of John Calvin? Once we have been received into God's new people by baptism, we are given everything that Jesus Christ is and has and are enabled to appropriate it in increasing measure by sharing Christ in the preaching of his Word, in the receiving of his Supper, in the liturgical life of his body, the Church" ("Reformed Spirituality," 71-72).

45. Flavel, *Works*, V:571.

46. Flavel, *Works*, V:568.

47. Flavel, *Works*, V:28.

of obedience, but none at all in point of reliance."[48] Simply put, believers must apply themselves to these means of grace while ultimately depending upon the Holy Spirit to reward their efforts.[49] And the Holy Spirit does so by granting: (1) "a real taste of the joy of the Lord"; (2) "a mighty strength and power," actuating the soul's "faculties and graces"; (3) "a remarkable transformation and change of spirit"; and (4) "a vigorous working of the heart heaven-ward; a mounting of the soul upward."[50] In short, the Holy Spirit impresses God's "influences" upon the soul so that its affections are stirred and it makes suitable "returns" to God.

---

48. Flavel, *Works*, V:571.
49. Flavel, *Works*, V:424.
50. Flavel, *Works*, VI:390.

Chapter 11

————— ((●)) —————

THE HOPE OF UNION
WITH CHRIST

Although communion with God in spiritual duties is precious, Flavel quickly acknowledges that it falls far short of
what awaits the believer in heaven:

> The believer knows, how sweet soever his communion
> with Christ is in this world, yet that communion he
> shall have with Christ in heaven, will far excel it: there
> it will be more intimate and immediate (1 Cor. 12:12),
> more full and perfect, even to satisfaction (Ps. 17:15),
> more constant and continued, not suffering such in-
> terruption as it doth here (Rev. 21:25), more pure and
> unmixed; here our corruptions work with our graces
> (Rom. 7:21), but there grace shall work alone: in a
> word, more durable and perpetual; we shall be ever
> with the Lord (1 Thess. 4:7).[1]

As Flavel makes clear, the presence of sin disrupts our
communion with God. At glorification, however, we will be
free from this burden. We will be like Christ and, therefore,
able to commune with God to the fullest capacity of our souls.
This will result in unparalleled delight, as our souls will rest
fully in Him. Flavel summarizes this hope, asking, "What is
the life of glory but the vision of God, and the soul's assimi-

---

1. Flavel, *Works*, VI:450. For "a six-fold difference betwixt the spiritual comforts of believers on earth, and the joys that are above," see
IV:228-89.

lation to God by that vision? From both which results that unspeakable joy and delight which passeth understanding."[2]

In this chapter, we turn to Flavel's concept of "the life of glory"—the hope of all those who are in Christ. I will demonstrate that it rests upon three related truths: the vision of God, the image of God, and the enjoyment of God.

The Vision of God

Beginning with the vision of God, Flavel makes it clear that we see God at present, in that we behold Him through the eyes of faith.[3] But this is nothing to be compared with what we will see in heaven. He remarks, "To see God in his word and works, is the happiness of the saints on earth; but to see him face to face, will be the fullness of their blessedness in heaven (1 John 3:2)."[4] Again, "Those weak and dim representations made by faith, at a distance, are the very joy and rejoicing of a believer's soul now (1 Pet. 1:7-8), but how sweet and transporting soever these visions of faith be, they are not worthy to be named in comparison with the immediate and beatifical vision (1 Cor. 13:12)."[5]

As for what it means to see God face to face, Flavel says that it is "to know him as he is...to see him so perfectly and fully, that the understanding can proceed no farther in point of knowledge, concerning that great question, *What is God?*"[6] For Flavel, this is not primarily a sight of the eye, but a sight of the soul. As Watson explains:

> But when I say our seeing of God in heaven is corporeal, my meaning is that we shall with bodily eyes behold Jesus Christ, through whom the glory of God,

---

2. Flavel, *Works*, II:95.

3. According to Flavel, men see Christ in three ways. (1) They see him "carnally" with an eye of "flesh" (Isa. 53:2). (2) They see him "fiducially" by the eye of "faith" (John 6:40). (3) They see him "beatifically" by the glorified eye (Job 19:26-27) (*Works*, VI:411-12).

4. Flavel, *Works*, II:282.

5. Flavel, *Works*, III:120.

6. Flavel, *Works*, III:47; also see III:120.

his wisdom, holiness, and mercy, shall shine forth to the soul. Put a back of steel to the glass and you may see a face in it. So the human nature of Christ is as it were a back of steel through which we may see the glory of God (2 Cor. 4:6). In this sense that scripture is to be understood, 'With these eyes I shall see God' (Job 19:26-27).[7]

William Perkins[8] is particularly helpful on this point. In the context of Christ's promise, "Blessed are the pure in heart: for they shall see God" (Matt. 5:8), he observes, "there is a two-fold sight in man."[9] The first is a sight of the eye, by which "no man can see God in his essence and substance, which is most spirituall, and so invisible; for the eye seeth nothing but things corporall and visible: a man by his eye cannot see his owne soul, and much lesse the substance of God." The second is a sight of the mind, by which we know God. This sight is imperfect in this life, in that the mind "knowes not Gods essence or substance, but onely by the effects; as by his word and Sacraments; and by his creatures."[10] In the life to come, however, this sight of the mind will be "perfect." We will be "filled" with the knowledge of God. Or, again, as Flavel describes it: our understanding will "proceed no farther in point of knowledge, concerning that great question, *What is God?*"

The Image of God

As a result of this beatifical vision, we will be changed. Flavel explains how. (1) It will be a "satisfying" sight.[11] David says,

---

7. Thomas Watson, *The Beatitudes* (1660; Edinburgh: Banner of Truth, 1994), 197.

8. William Perkins (1558-1602) was a professor at Christ's College, Cambridge. He was one of the most influential figures in the rise and development of English Reformed theology.

9. William Perkins, *A Godly and Learned Exposition upon Christ's Sermon on the Mount* in *The Works of William Perkins* (London, 1631), III:15.

10. Perkins, *Christ's Sermon on the Mount*, III:16.

11. Flavel, *Works*, III:121.

"As for me, I will behold thy face in righteousness: I shall be satisfied, when I awake, with thy likeness" (Ps. 17:15). For Flavel, this means that "the understanding can know no more, the will can will no more; the affections of joy, delight, and love are at full rest and quiet in their proper centre."[12] In a word, "God may be all in all" (1 Cor. 15:28). (2) It will be an "appropriating" sight.[13] This means that we will see God as *our* God. As Job cries, "In my flesh shall I see God: whom I shall see for myself, and mine eyes shall behold, and not another" (Job 19:26-27). On the judgment day, all men will stand before God. For unbelievers, it will be a cause of dread, because they will have no personal interest in God. For believers, however, it will be a cause of joy, because they will see *their* God. (3) It will be a "deeply affecting" sight.[14] As Paul writes, "For our conversation is in heaven; from whence also we look for the Saviour, the Lord Jesus Christ; who shall change our vile body, that it may be fashioned like unto his glorious body" (Phil. 3:20-21). That sight will change us forever, in that it will result in "perfect freedom from sin."[15] (4) It will be an "everlasting" sight.[16] Paul writes, "Then we which are alive and remain shall be caught up together with them in the clouds, to meet the Lord in the air: and so shall we ever be with the Lord" (1 Thess. 4:17). This sight will never come to an end, but will hold the believer's attention for all eternity. Flavel declares, "If one hour's enjoyment of God, in the way of faith, be so sweet, and no price can be put upon it, nothing on earth taken in exchange for it; what must a whole eternity, in the immediate and full visions of that blessed face in heaven be!"[17]

---

12. Flavel, *Works*, III:121.
13. Flavel, *Works*, III:121.
14. Flavel, *Works*, III:122.
15. Flavel, *Works*, VI:207; also see VI:215.
16. Flavel, *Works*, III:122.
17. Flavel, *Works*, III:122.

In short, the beatifical vision means that the image of God will be restored in us. The faculties of the soul will again be marked by knowledge, righteousness, and holiness. The mind will perceive God as the greatest good, and the affections will love God as the greatest good. God will impress His glory upon the soul to its fullest capacity, and it will make suitable returns to Him.

The Enjoyment of God

These "returns" are summed up in the enjoyment of God. According to Flavel, there is a three-fold happiness to be enjoyed in heaven. (1) The "objective" happiness is God Himself.[18] "If it could be supposed...that God should withdraw from the saints in heaven, and say, Take heaven, and divide it among you; but as for me, I will withdraw from you; the saints would fall a weeping in heaven, and say, Lord, take heaven, and give it to whom thou wilt; it is no heaven to us, except thou be there." (2) The "subjective" happiness is "the attemperation and suiting of the soul and body to God."[19] "It consists in removing from both all that is indecent, and inconsistent with a state of such complete glory and happiness, and in superinducting and clothing it with all heavenly qualities."[20] (3) The "formal" happiness is "the fullness of satisfaction resulting from the blessed sight and enjoyment of God, by a soul so attempered to him."[21] "Ah, what a happiness is here! To look and love, to drink and sing, and drink again at the fountain head of the highest glory!"[22]

---

18. Flavel, *Works*, I:193.

19. Flavel, *Works*, I:193.

20. Flavel, *Works*, I:194.

21. Flavel, *Works*, I:194.

22. Flavel, *Works*, I:195. It is true that the believer enjoys God at present; however, that delight pales in comparison to what is coming. Why? (1) "The spiritual pleasures the soul hath in the body, are but by reflection; but those it enjoys out of the body, are by immediate intuition." (2) "The pleasures it now hath, though they be of a

Upon seeing God, the soul will be renewed in the image of God. This renewal will enable the soul to find its complete rest in God. And this will be the believer's heaven. "Four things," notes Flavel, "disturb the souls of believers in this world": afflictions, temptations, corruptions, and absence from God. He adds, "If the three former causes of disquietness were totally removed, so that a believer were placed in such a condition upon earth, where no affliction could disturb him, no temptation trouble him, no corruption defile or grieve him, yet his very absence from God must still keep him restless and unsatisfied."[23] The believer's hope is that one day he will be with his God, in whose "presence is fullness of joy," and at whose "right hand there are pleasures for evermore" (Ps. 16:11).

Conclusion

"What is the chief end of man?" asks the *Westminster Shorter Catechism*. The answer: "Man's chief end is to glorify God, and to enjoy him forever."[24] As Flavel puts it, "God is that supreme good, in the enjoyment of whom all true happiness lies."[25] Again, "Communion with God, and the enjoyment

---

divine nature, yet they are relished by the vitiated appetite of a sick and distempered soul." (3) "The pleasures of a gracious soul on earth are but rare and seldom, meeting with many and long interruptions." (4) "The highest pleasures of a gracious soul in the body, are but the pleasures of an uncentered soul." To sum up, Flavel says that the soul's pleasures at present "are but the pleasures of hope and expectation, which cannot bear any proportion to those of sight and full fruition" (*Works*, III:45). When believers see God face-to-face, they will experience pleasure to the fullest. "This immediate knowledge and sight of God face to face, will be infinitely more sweet, and ravishingly pleasant than any, or all the views we had of him here by faith ever were, or possibly could be" (*Works*, III:48; also see VI:215).

23. Flavel, *Works*, II:284.

24. For Flavel's treatment of the first question of the *Westminster Shorter Catechism*, see *Works*, VI:141-42.

25. Flavel, *Works*, V:210; also see II:533.

of him, are the true and proper intentions and purposes for which the soul of man was created."[26] God created us to glorify Him; we glorify Him by delighting in Him; and we delight in Him by communing with Him. The image of God is the means by which we do this. At glorification, that image will be fully restored. And this is the hope of union with Christ.

---

26. Flavel, *Works*, II:533.

CONCLUSION

⊸⊶⟨(•)⟩⊶⊸

My purpose in this book has been to consider why Flavel views the doctrine of the believer's mystical union with Christ as an "admirable and astonishing mystery."[1] As mentioned in the introduction, I embarked on this study, hoping that it would contribute to a greater admiration for this pastor-theologian, a greater understanding of Puritan spirituality, a greater appreciation of what it means to be "mystically united to the Lord of glory," and a greater burning of the heart "in love to Christ." I leave it to the reader to decide if I have succeeded.

By way of conclusion, I simply want to draw our attention to Calvin's warning that theology "is not apprehended by the understanding and memory alone, as other disciplines are, but it is received only when it possesses the whole soul, and finds a seat and resting place in the inmost affection of the heart."[2] The Puritans (including Flavel) would agree wholeheartedly. As Martyn Lloyd-Jones notes, "There is nothing that they more deplored than a mere academic, intellectual, theoretical view of the Truth."[3] David Sceats concurs, "Puritans would hardly have acknowledged the notion of 'pure theology' and would have been distinctly uncomfortable with the idea that theology might have been studied as an academic discipline without reference to its situational application."[4] The Puritan approach is entrenched in the

---

1. Flavel, *Works*, II:239.

2. Calvin, *Institutes*, III.VI.4.

3. Lloyd-Jones, *The Puritans,* 55.

4. David Sceats, "The Experience of Grace: Aspects of the Faith and Spirituality of the Puritans," *Grove Spirituality Series* 62 (1997): 12.

words of William Ames,[5] "Theology is the doctrine or teaching of living to God."[6]

This emphasis upon "living to God" is particularly relevant when it comes to the believer's mystical union with Christ. In a word, this doctrine must be manifested in life. As Handley Moule remarks, "To grasp this deep yet simple fact [i.e., union with Christ] is to pour into the heart, and through it into the life, in all its parts, a new light, a new power."[7] Similarly, Martyn Lloyd-Jones writes, "If you have got hold of this idea you will have discovered the most glorious truth you will ever know in your life."[8]

Flavel certainly had a hold of it, and it did indeed pour from his heart into his life. For this reason, I can think of no better way to conclude than with the following heartfelt application from this man of God:

> *First*, How contented and well pleased should we be with our outward lot, however providence hath cast it for us in this world! O do not repine, God hath dealt bountifully with you; upon others he hath bestowed the good things of this world; upon you, himself in Christ.... *Secondly*, How humble and lowly in spirit should you be under your great advancement! It is true, God hath magnified you greatly by this union, but yet do not swell.... You shine, but it is as the stars, with a borrowed light.... *Thirdly*, How zealous should you be to honour Christ, who hath put so much honour upon you! Be willing to give glory to Christ, though his glory

---

5. William Ames (1576-1633) was a graduate of Christ's College, Cambridge. Because of his Puritan convictions, he left England for Holland in 1610. He became a professor at the University of Franeker.

6. William Ames, *Medulla Theologiae (The Marrow of Theology)* translated from the third Latin edition by J. D. Eusden, 1629; (Grand Rapids: Baker Books, 1997), I.I.1.

7. Moule, *Thoughts on Union with Christ*, 15-16.

8. Martyn Lloyd-Jones, *Romans – The Law: Its Function and Limits: Exposition of 7:1-8:4* (Grand Rapids: Zondervan, 1973), 277.

should rise out of your shame.... *Fourthly*, How exact and circumspect should you be in all your ways, remembering whose you are, and whom you represent! Shall it be said, that a member of Christ was convicted of unrighteousness and unholy actions!... *Fifthly*, How studious should you be of peace among yourselves, who are so nearly united to such a Head, and thereby are made fellow-members of the same body!... *Sixthly*, and lastly, How joyful and comfortable should you be, to whom Christ, with all his treasures and benefits, is effectually applied in this blessed union of your souls with him! This brings him into your possession: O how great! how glorious a person do these little weak arms of our faith embrace!

Thanks be to God for Jesus Christ.

Bibliography

I. Primary Sources

Ames, W. *Medulla Theologiae (The Marrow of Theology)* translated from the third Latin edition by J. D. Eusden, 1629; (Grand Rapids: Baker Books, 1997).

Augustine. *The City of God* in *A Select Library of the Nicene and Post-Nicene Fathers of the Christian Church: Vol. I-VIII*, ed. P. Schaff (New York: Random House, 1948).

Baxter, R. *The Divine Life* in *The Practical Works of Richard Baxter: Select Treatises* (London: Blackie & Son, 1863; rpt., Grand Rapids: Baker Book House, 1981).

Calvin, J. *The Epistle of the Apostle Paul to the Romans* in *Calvin's Commentaries Vol. I-XXII* (Grand Rapids: Baker Books, 2003).

_____. *Institutes of the Christian Religion* in *The Library of Christian Classics: Vol. XX-XXI*, ed. J. T. McNeill (Philadelphia: Westminster Press, 1960).

_____. *The Bondage and Liberation of the Will*, ed. A. N. S. Lane (Grand Rapids: Baker Books, 1996).

Charnock, S. *Discourses Upon the Existence and Attributes of God: Vol. I-II* (London: Robert Carter & Brothers, 1853; rpt., Grand Rapids: Baker Books, 1990).

_____. *Discourses Upon Regeneration* in *The Works of Stephen Charnock: Vol. III*, ed. J. Nichol (London, 1865; rpt., Edinburgh: Banner of Truth, 1986).

Flavel, J. *The Works of John Flavel: Vol. I-VI* (London: W. Baynes and Son, 1820; rpt., London: Banner of Truth, 1968).

A Caution to Seamen: A Dissuasive against Several Horrid and Detestable Sins.

A Coronation Sermon.

A Familiar Conference between a Minister and a Doubting Christian Concerning the Sacrament of the Lord's Supper.

A Hymn upon Romans 5:6-11.

A Narrative of some late and wonderful Sea Deliverances.

An Exposition of the Westminster Assembly's Shorter Catechism.

Antipharmacum Saluberrimum: A Serious and Seasonable Caveat to all the Saints in this Hour of Temptation.

A Practical Treatise on Fear: Its Varieties, Uses, Causes, Effects, and Remedies.

A Saint Indeed; or, The Great Work of a Christian Explained and Applied.

A Sermon Preached at the Funeral of John Upton, of Lupton (Devon).

A Token for Mourners.

A Two-column Table of the Sins and Duties attaching to Church Membership.

Divine Conduct; or, The Mystery of Providence: A Treatise upon Psalm 57:2.

England's Duty under the Present Gospel Liberty (1689).

Gospel Unity Recommended to the Churches of Christ.

Husbandry Spiritualized: The Heavenly Use of Earthly Things.

Mount Pisgah: A Sermon preached at the Public Thanksgiving, February 14, 1688-9, for England's Delivery from Popery.

Navigation Spiritualized: A New Compass for Seamen.

Pneumatologia: A Treatise of the Soul of Man.

Preparations for Suffering; or, the Best Work in the Worst Times.

Saint Indeed; or, The Great Work of a Christian, Opened and Pressed.

The Balm of the Covenant applied to the Bleeding Wounds of Afflicted Saints.

The Character of an Evangelical Pastor drawn by Christ.

The Fountain of Life; or, A Display of Christ in His Essential and Mediatorial Glory.

The Method of Grace in the Gospel Redemption.

The Occasions, Causes, Nature, Rise, Growth and Remedies of Mental Errors.

The Reasonableness of Personal Reformation and the Necessity of Conversion.

The Righteous Man's Refuge.

The Seamen's Companion: Six Sermons on the Mysteries of Providence as relating to Seamen; and the Sins, Dangers, Duties and Troubles of Seamen.

The Touchstone of Sincerity; or, The Signs of Grace and the Symptoms of Hypocrisy.

Tidings from Rome of England's Alarm.

Twelve Sacramental Meditations.

Vindiciae Legis et Foederis; or, A Reply to Mr Philip Cary's Solemn Call in which He Contends Against the Right of Believers' Infants to Baptism.

Hall, J. *Christ Mystical; or, The Blessed Union of Christ and His Members* (London: Hodder and Stoughton, 1893).

Marshall, W. *The Gospel Mystery of Sanctification* (1670; Grand Rapids: Reformation Heritage Books, 1999).

Owen, J. *The Works of John Owen: Vol. I-XVI*, ed. W. H. Gould (London: Johnstone & Hunter, 1850; rpt., Edinburgh: Banner of Truth, 1977).

Pearse, E. *The Best Match; or, The Soul's Espousal to Christ* (Morgan: Soli Deo Gloria, 1994).

Perkins, W. *A Godly and Learned Exposition upon Christ's Sermon on the Mount* in *The Works of William Perkins: Vol. III* (London, 1631).

Swinnock, G. *The Works of George Swinnock: Vol. I-V*, ed. James Nichol (London, 1868; rpt., Edinburgh: Banner of Truth, 1992).

Watson, T. *A Body of Divinity Contained in Sermons Upon the Westminster Assembly's Catechism* (1692; 1890; rpt., London: Banner of Truth, 1958).

————. *All Things for Good; or, The Divine Cordial* (1663; Edinburgh: Banner of Truth, 1986; rpt., 1994).

_____. *The Beatitudes* (1660; Edinburgh: Banner of Truth, 1994).

II. Secondary Sources

Armstrong, B. *Calvinism and the Amyraut Heresy: Protestant Scholasticism and Humanism in Seventeenth-Century France* (University of Wisconsin Press, 1969).

Beeke, J. R. *Assurance of Faith: Calvin, English Puritanism, and the Dutch Second Reformation* (New York: Peter Lang, 1991).

_____. *Puritan Reformed Spirituality* (Grand Rapids: Reformation Heritage Books, 2004).

_____, and R. Pederson. *Meet the Puritans* (Grand Rapids: Reformation Heritage Books, 2006).

Bell, C. "Calvin and the Extent of the Atonement," *Evangelical Quarterly* 55 (1983): 115-23.

Boersma, H. "Calvin and the Extent of the Atonement," *Evangelical Quarterly* 64 (1992): 333-55.

Breward, I. "The Abolition of Puritanism," *Journal of Religious History* 7 (1972): 20-34.

Christianson, P. "Reformers and the Church of England under Elizabeth I and the Early Stuarts," *Journal of Ecclesiastical History* 31 (1980): 463-82.

Collinson, P. "A Comment: Concerning the Name Puritan," *Journal of Ecclesiastical History* 31 (1980): 483-88.

Coolidge, J. S. *The Pauline Renaissance in England: Puritanism and the Bible* (Oxford: Clarendon Press, 1970).

Ferguson, S. B. *John Owen on the Christian Life* (Edinburgh: Banner of Truth, 1987).

Finlayson, M. G. "Puritanism and Puritans: Labels or Libels?" *Canadian Journal of History* 8 (1973): 203-23.

Gerrish, B. A. *Grace and Gratitude: The Eucharist Theology of John Calvin* (Minneapolis: Fortress Press, 1993).

_____. "The Lord's Supper in the Reformed Confessions," *Theology Today* 23 (1966): 224-43.

Godfrey, W. R. "Reformed Thought on the Extent of the Atonement to 1618," *Westminster Theological Journal* 37 (1975): 133-71.

Griffiths, S. *Redeem the Time: Sin in the Writings of John Owen* (Ross-shire: Christian Focus, 2001).

Gwyn-Thomas, J. "The Puritan Doctrine of Christian Joy" in *Puritan Papers: Vol. II*, ed. J. I. Packer (Phillipsburg: Presbyterian and Reformed, 2001), 119-240.

Hageman, H. G. "Reformed Spirituality" in *Protestant Spiritual Traditions*, ed. F. C. Senn (New York: Paulist, 1986), 55-79.

Hall, B. "Calvin Against the Calvinists" in *John Calvin: A Collection of Distinguishing Essays*, ed. G. E. Duffield (Grand Rapids: Eerdmans, 1966), 19-37.

_____. "Puritanism: The Problem of Definition" in *Humanists and Protestants: 1500-1900* (Edinburgh: T & T Clark, 1990), 237-54.

Helm, P. *Calvin and the Calvinists* (Edinburgh: Banner of Truth, 1982).

Hesselink, I. J. *Calvin's Concept of the Law* (Allison Park: Pickwick Publications, 1992).

Hill, C. *Society and Puritanism in Pre-Revolutionary England* (London: Panther Books, 1969).

Hoekema, A. "The Covenant of Grace in Calvin's Teaching," *Calvin Theological Journal* 2 (1967): 133-61.

Hoitenga, D. *John Calvin and the Will: A Critique and Corrective* (Grand Rapids: Baker Books, 1997).

Jewett, P. K. "Concerning the Allegorical Interpretation of Scripture," *Westminster Theological Journal* 17 (1954): 1-20.

Jones, R. T. "Union With Christ: The Existential Nerve of Puritan Piety," *Tyndale Bulletin* 41 (1990): 186-208.

Kendall, R. T. *Calvin and English Calvinism to 1649* (Oxford University Press, 1979).

_____. "The Puritan Modification of Calvin's Theology" in *John Calvin: His Influence in the Western World*, ed. W. S. Reid (Grand Rapids: Zondervan, 1982), 199-214.

Kevan, E. F. *The Grace of Law* (Ligonier: Soli Deo Gloria, 1993).

Lane, A. N. S. "Did Calvin Believe in Free Will?" *Vox Evangelica* 12 (1981): 72-90.

Lee, S. (ed.) *Dictionary of National Biography* (London: Smith, Elder & Co., 1909).

Leith, J. H. *John Calvin's Doctrine of the Christian Life* (Louisville: John Knox Press, 1989).

Letham, R. "Faith and Assurance in Early Calvinism: A Model of Continuity and Diversity" in *Later Calvinism: International Perspectives*, ed. W. F. Graham (Kirksville: Sixteenth Century Journal, 1992), 355-84.

————. "The *Foedus Operum*: Some Factors Accounting for its Development," *The Sixteenth Century Journal* 14 (1983): 457-67.

Lewis, P. *The Genius of Puritanism* (Morgan: Soli Deo Gloria, 1996).

Lillback, P. *The Binding of God: Calvin's Role in the Development of Covenant Theology* (Grand Rapids: Baker Books, 2001).

Lloyd-Jones, M. *Romans—The Law: Its Function and Limits: Exposition of 7:1-8:4* (Grand Rapids: Zondervan, 1973).

————. *The Puritans: Their Origins and Successors* (Edinburgh: Banner of Truth, 2002).

Lovelace, R. C. "The Anatomy of Puritan Piety: English Puritan Devotional Literature, 1600-1640" in *Christian Spirituality III*, eds. L. Dupré and D. E. Saliers (New York: Crossroad Publishing, 1989), 294-323.

Marsden, G. M. "Perry Miller's Rehabilitation of the Puritans: A Critique" in *Reckoning With the Past: Historical Essays on American Evangelicalism from the Institute for the Study of American Evangelicals*, ed. D. G. Hart (Grand Rapids: Baker Books, 1995), 23-38.

McGee, J. S. *The Godly Man in Stuart England: Anglicans, Puritans, and the Two Tables, 1620-1670* (Yale University Press, 1976).

McGiffert, M. "The Perkinsian Moment of Federal Theology," *Calvin Theological Journal* 29 (1994): 117-148.

McSorley, H. J. *Luther: Right or Wrong? An Ecumenical-Theological Study of Luther's Major Work, The Bondage of the Will* (New York: Newman Press, 1969).

Miller, P. *The New England Mind: The Seventeenth Century* (Harvard University Press, 1963).

Moule, H. *Thoughts on Union with Christ* (London: Seeley & Co. Limited, 1885).

Muller, R. *Christ and the Decree: Christology and Predestination in Reformed Theology from Calvin to Perkins* (Grand Rapids: Baker Books, 1986).

————. "*Fides* and *Cognitio* in Relation to the Problem of Intellect and Will in the Theology of John Calvin," *Calvin Theological Journal* 25 (1990): 207-24.

Murray, J. *Principles of Conduct* (Grand Rapids: Eerdmans, 1957).

Nicole, R. "John Calvin's View of the Extent of the Atonement," *Westminster Theological Journal* 47 (1985): 197-225.

Packer, J. I. *A Quest for Godliness: The Puritan Vision of the Christian Life* (Wheaton: Crossway Books, 1990).

————. *Knowing God* (London, Hodder and Stoughton, 1975).

Partee, C. "Calvin's Central Dogma Again," *Sixteenth Century Journal* 18 (1987): 191-199.

Pettit, N. *The Heart Prepared: Grace and Conversion in Puritan Spiritual Life* (Middletown: Wesleyan University Press, 1989).

Rolston, H. *John Calvin Versus the Westminster Confession* (Richmond: John Knox Press, 1972).

Sceats, D. "The Experience of Grace: Aspects of the Faith and Spirituality of the Puritans," *Grove Spirituality Series* 62 (1997).

Strehle, S. "The Extent of the Atonement and the Synod of Dort," *Westminster Theological Journal* 51 (1989): 1-23.

Thomas, D. *Proclaiming the Incomprehensible God: Calvin's Teaching on Job* (Ross-shire: Christian Focus, 2004).

Thomas, M. *The Extent of the Atonement: A Dilemma for Reformed Theology from Calvin to the Consensus (1536 to 1675)* (Bletchley: Paternoster, 1997).

Toon, P. *From Mind to Heart: Christian Meditation Today* (Grand Rapids: Baker Books, 1987).

Torrance, T. F. *Calvin's Doctrine of Man* (Grand Rapids: Eerdmans, 1957).

Trinterud, L. "The Origins of Puritanism," *Church History* 20 (1951): 37-57.

Tylenda, J. N. "Calvin and Christ's Presence in the Supper – True or Real," *Scottish Journal of Theology* 27 (1974): 65-75.

Whitney, D. S. *Spiritual Disciplines for the Christian Life* (Colorado Springs: NavPress, 1991).

Yuille, J. S. "How Pastoral is Open Theism? A Critique from the Writings of George Swinnock and Stephen Charnock," *Themelios* 32 (2007): 46-61.

_____. "Puritan Meditation: The Gateway from the Head to the Heart," *Eusebeia: The Bulletin of the Jonathan Edwards Centre for Reformed Spirituality* 4 (2005): 7-16.

Index

MEET THE PURITANS
With A Guide to Modern Reprints

Joel R. Beeke and Randall J. Pederson
978-1-60178-000-3   Hardback, 935 pages

Meet the Puritans provides a biographical and theological introduction to the Puritans whose works have been reprinted in the last fifty years, and also gives helpful summaries and insightful analyses of those reprinted works. It contains nearly 150 biographical entries, and nearly 700 summaries of reprinted works.

"A SWEET FLAME"
Piety in the Letters of Jonathan Edwards

Michael A. G. Haykin (ed.)
978-1-60178-011-9   Paperback, 184 pages

"A Sweet Flame" introduces readers to the piety of Jonathan Edwards (1703-1758). Dr. Haykin's biographical sketch of Edwards captures the importance the New England minister placed on Scripture, family piety, and the church's reliance upon God. The remainder of the book presents 26 selections from various letters written by Edwards, two written by family members at his death, and an appendix drawing upon Edwards's last will and the inventory of his estate.